22 5/17 9/17

Living with a
Wild God

ALSO BY BARBARA EHRENREICH

Living with a Wild God

A NONBELIEVER'S SEARCH
FOR THE TRUTH ABOUT EVERYTHING

BARBARA EHRENREICH

TWELVE

New York Boston

Twelve
Hachette Book Group
237 Park Avenue
New York, NY 10017

www.HachetteBookGroup.com

Printed in the United States of America

RRD-C

First Edition: April 2014
10 9 8 7 6 5 4 3 2 1

Twelve is an imprint of Grand Central Publishing.
The Twelve name and logo are trademarks of Hachette Book Group, Inc.

The Hachette Speakers Bureau provides a wide range of authors for speaking events. To find out more, go to www.hachettespeakersbureau.com or call (866) 376-6591.

The publisher is not responsible for websites (or their content) that are not owned by the publisher.

Library of Congress Cataloging-in-Publication Data
Ehrenreich, Barbara.
  Living with a Wild God : a memoir / Barbara Ehrenreich.
    pages cm
  ISBN 978-1-4555-0176-2 (hardback) — ISBN 978-1-4789-0027-6 (audiobook) — ISBN 978-1-61113-808-5 (audio download) 1. Ehrenreich, Barbara. 2. Women authors, American—Biography. 3. Self-actualization (Psychology)—Biography. 4. Philosophy and religion—Biography. I. Title.
  PS3555.H65Z46 2014
  813'.54—dc23
  [B]
                              2013038766

For Anna and Clara, Rosa and Ben.

CONTENTS

FOREWORD

In the spring of 2001, I was presented with the unnerving task of assembling my papers for storage in a university library. The timing of this forced review of my life, or at least its paper vestiges, could not have been more viciously appropriate, since I was in the midst of treatment for breast cancer and facing the possibility of a somewhat earlier death than seemed fair for anyone as fit and outdoorsy as myself. A librarian had come down from Cambridge to help, and we spread the stacks of papers out on the largest available surface—the pool table that had been left behind on the screened-in porch by a departed boyfriend. There were the drafts of unpublished manifestos, notebooks filled with jottings on human history and evolution, polemical exchanges on the relationship between feminism and other social movements, a few diplomas and awards for academic achievements, and a small trove of letters from long-gone lovers.

I felt very little curiosity about these items or even much sense of ownership. If you had asked me whether my life so far had any narrative arc or even consistent themes, I would have had to say no, not that I could make out. It seemed to me I had spent a lot of time careening from one thing to another—from science to journalism, for example, and from journalism to the manic scholarship on display in my more historical works, not to mention the different romantic relationships and the many oscillations between activism and quiet study. I had—and still have—no inclination to try to patch this all together into a single story. I will never write an autobiography, nor am I sure, after all these years, that there is even one coherent "self" or "voice" to serve as narrator.

The impetus for packing off the papers was simply the climate in the lower Florida Keys, where I was living at the time, and which is, over the long run, fatally hostile to paper of any kind. When the library approached me I had been disappointed that they weren't offering any money, because I hadn't received a very munificent advance for my forthcoming book, *Nickel and Dimed*, and had in the course of the illness resorted to borrowing money from friends. But if a distinguished library wanted to provide an air-conditioned, dehumidified dwelling place for these fragments and notes, fine. I figured that maybe someday—if civilization, represented by universities and libraries, endured long enough—a future graduate student might find something of interest in the boxes we were rapidly filling, say for a dissertation on little-known aspects of the grassroots intellectual ferment within the feminist movement of the seventies.

There was only one thing I held back from the outgoing cardboard boxes—a thick reddish folder or envelope of the old-fashioned kind, tied by a string. It had survived for about forty-eight years through god knows how many moves from state to state and one apartment to another. In all that time I had never opened it and never mentioned or referred to it. But somehow I had always remembered to pack it in the bottom of a suitcase, no matter how chaotic the circumstances of the move. Future graduate students could snicker over my love affairs and political idealism if they were so minded, but they could not have this.

The folder contains a kind of journal, though it is really only an intermittent series of entries, each on a separate piece of paper, from the years 1956 to 1966, and mostly from the first three of those years, starting when I was fourteen. What impelled me to hold it back from the tomb that was about to swallow all the other paper remnants of my life was the prospect of mortality—though not my own mortality as a fifty-nine-year-old woman with a full, productive life behind her. In fact, if you're not prepared to die when you're almost sixty, then I would say you've been falling down on your philosophical responsibilities as a grown-up human being. As for the manner of my death, I would have preferred to start swimming out across the Gulf at dusk, which is shark feeding time, and was still hoping to squeeze that in, should the cancer take a turn for the worse.

No, what scared me on that clear, breezy spring day was the knowledge that the journal is not a self-explanatory, stand-alone document. It begins, promisingly enough, on a wry note:

Today, July fourth, 1956, is a national holiday. That means that people who would normally work elsewhere are now free to work at home. Independence Day is celebrated all over the nation by noisy declarations of disregard for all laws prohibiting firecrackers.

But too often it is tangled and evasive, especially on some of the most important things, which as a girl I had found too private and too searing to commit to paper. I knew the journal would require a major job of exegesis, a strenuous reconstruction of all that I once thought was better left unsaid. So the sad thing was that if I—the fifty-nine-year-old Barbara—died, *she* died too: the girl who had written these things so long ago. That's who, or what, I was determined to save, because if I have any core identity, any central

theme that has survived all the apparent changes of subject, the secret of it lies with her.

I knew, roughly speaking, what was in the journal, and that it
records what led up to an event so strange, so cataclysmic, that I
never in all the intervening years wrote or spoke about it. I did
make an attempt once or twice with someone I was especially close
to, only to have them change the subject or look away uneasily.
What had happened did not occupy any category that intersected
with my central adult concerns, such as making a living and taking care of my family while at the same time doing what little I
could to try to reduce the amount of cruelty in the world. Besides,
despite what I like to think of as continual improvements in my
ability to express myself, when it came to this one topic, there were
no words.

It hadn't been until I reached my forties that I discovered that
what happened to me, or something very similar, has also happened to many other people, and that some of them had even
found ways of talking about it, although usually in a vocabulary
and framework foreign to me, if not actually repulsive. The conventional term is "mystical experience," meaning something that
by its very nature lies beyond the reach of language, except for
some vague verbal hand-wavings about "mystery" and "transcendence." As far as I was concerned—as a rationalist, an atheist, a
scientist by training—this was the realm of gods and fairies and of
no use to the great human project of trying to retain a foothold on
the planet for future generations.

So what do you do with something like this—an experience so
anomalous, so disconnected from the normal life you share with
other people, that you can't even figure out how to talk about
it? I was also, I have to admit, afraid of sounding crazy. Try in-
serting an account of a mystical experience into a conversation

and you'll likely get the same response as you would if you con-
fided that you had been the victim of an alien abduction. Both
involve encounters with beings whose existence is not universally
acknowledged—extraterrestrial beings in the one case, spirits,
deities, or some Universal Being in the other—and in the academic literature, both are subjected to the same sort of clinical
condescension. For example, a recent anthology on "anomalous
experiences" from the American Psychological Association includes very similar chapters on alien abductions and mystical experiences, each offering a highly clinical discussion of "prevalence,"
"predisposing factors," "biological markers," and so forth, as well
as a variety of possible psychiatric explanations. You might as well
admit to seeing ghosts or hearing disembodied voices.

It is true, I should further admit, that the narrative as I have
reconstructed it lends itself quite readily to psychiatric explanation, or explanations: the tense and sometimes hazardous family
life, the secret childhood quest for cosmic knowledge, the eerie
lapses into a kind of "second sight," the spectacular breakdown in
my late teens. If I did not want to get dragged back down by any
of the stickier parts of this, I would have to become almost a new
person—neither my young self nor my older self, but a sternly objective reporter seeking truth from both. And I did not want to get
dragged back down.

For all these reasons, it took several years after I salvaged the
journal in 2001 before I realized this was something I could no
longer dodge. I would get started—reading the journal and making notes to myself on the context of the entries and the events
that had been omitted from them—only to turn aside for some
far more urgent matter in the real world of living, suffering other
people, compared to which this project seemed inexcusably self-
involved. In 2005 I forced myself to transcribe the entire thing,

typing about an hour a day for a couple of weeks, and that was when I came across this, written in July 1958:

> I write this from a sense of duty, a feeling of obligation to my future self, whom I implore to read with compassion. What will I be, the person who, months [or, as it turned out, decades] later reads this? Myself, the same as ever? What have you learned since you wrote this?

There was no escaping it: That long-ago girl had chosen *me*— the grown-up and now aging person I have become—to carry on her work.

CHAPTER 1

The Situation

Sometime in my thirteenth year, but a little before I actually achieved that age, things began to assemble themselves into what I called "the situation." By this I did not mean anything peculiar to myself—from the conditions of my family to the historical moment—but things more generally shared by humankind: ecstatic springtimes and bitter winters, swirlings and shrinkings, yearning and terror. All followed by death.

At this point I set my goal for life, which was to find out why. What is the point of our brief existence? What are we doing here and to what end? I had no plan of attack because I had no notion of what form the answer might take or where it might be found. Would it be in a book or in a place? Coded or in plain sight? Would it take years of patient study to comprehend or would it come in a rush of revelation? And if it was easily available, say in a library book, why didn't anyone ever mention it? Because one thing you learn early in this line of work is that you can't go around telling people, "I'm on a mission to discover the purpose of life." Not if you're hoping to prolong the conversation.

I read everything I could lay my hands on, from popularized

science to the Romantic poets, and just in case the answer lay all around me in some more hidden form, I looked for patterns everywhere—anagrams, number sequences, clusters, and coincidences. I still do these things and tend to think of them as a normal requirement of the waking state: counting whatever items present themselves, checking for prime numbers, monitoring for tiny trends in the number of birds or the passage of cars as seen from a hotel window, inventing elaborate backstories for everyone I encounter.

The one place I never thought to look for answers was religion. That approach had been foreclosed at some point in the late nineteenth century when, according to my father, his grandmother Mamie McLaughlin renounced the Catholic faith. When her father was dying she had sent for a priest, only to get word back many hours later that the priest would come for no less than twenty-five dollars. Perhaps the priest could be forgiven for dodging the long ride by horse or mule to whatever makeshift, mudbound mining camp she and her family lived in. But Mamie did not forgive him. When she herself lay dying in childbirth a few years later, the priest, who may have been in the neighborhood anyway this time, showed up unbidden and started administering the last rites. At which point, as my father told the story, she used her last ounce of strength to hurl the crucifix off her chest and across the room.

How much of this story is true I don't know, but the fact that he liked to tell it testifies to the strength of my father's undying antagonism to religion. When he was a boy he had used some subterfuge to get a peek at the atheist texts kept out of public view in the Butte library, and when he grew up he bought himself a set of the complete works of Robert Ingersoll, the late-nineteenth-century American atheist lecturer, and sometimes bored us by reading aloud from these on Sunday mornings. What he could not have guessed and I only dimly understood at first was that his insistence on utter rationality could cut the other way and eventually lead to doubts about the entire system that my parents held up as "reality."

So I did not come to atheism the hard way, by risking the blows of nuns and irate parents, and maybe I would have been more steadfast if I had. I was born to atheism and raised in it, by people who had derived their own atheism from a proud tradition of working-class rejection of authority in all its forms, whether vested in bosses or priests, gods or demons. This is what defined my people, my tribe: We did not *believe*, and what this meant, when I started on the path of metaphysical questioning, was that there were no ready answers at hand. My religious friends—and my friends were almost all Catholics or Protestants or occasionally something more exotic like Jewish or Greek Orthodox—were convinced that God had a "plan" for us, and since God was good, it was a good plan, which we were required to endorse even without having any idea what it was. Just sign the paperwork; in other words, don't overintellectualize.

My parents never discouraged me from accompanying friends to religious services or events, and even once a sorry weekend of Baptist summer camp. I'd like to think they understood that any encounters with religion as actually practiced would only deepen my disbelief, but it may be that they just weren't noticing. When I was very young, still in the single-digit ages, I went with my friend Gail to her summer Bible class, where the instructor wound up the lesson by asking everyone to raise their hands if they had "acknowledged Jesus Christ as [their] personal savior." My hand stayed down, not because I was so honest but because I was afraid of follow-up questions about, for example, the details of my "acknowledgment" and to whom it had been addressed. What was she asking—that we not only accept the world as it is, but that we should be *grateful* for it? So the instructor kept me after class, although this was, for Christ's sake, only Bible class—and filled me in on the torments sweet Jesus had in store for an unsaved child. I wasn't frightened by her vision of hell, only anxious about how long she intended to hold me captive, because there was no way for a child to get past a looming grown-up and out the door.

It wasn't easy being a child atheist during the great Cold War or, for that matter, probably any time in human history outside of a few short-lived communist states. At school, I tried to blend in by mouthing the Lord's Prayer along with everyone else, which was mandatory in those days in the public schools, only sometimes permitting myself to slip into inaudible mocking gibberish. But I couldn't hide my peculiarity on Wednesday afternoons, when all the other kids were bused off to "religious study" at various churches while I remained behind at my desk under the grudging supervision of a teacher who might otherwise have been free to leave. There were times when I was taunted after school for being a "communist," which I understood only as a derogatory term for "atheist." Once some boys picked up rocks and chased me home, but I outran them.

How would I have turned out if I had not been set apart by this irreconcilable difference, if when I first started asking *why*, I had been given that great non-answer, "God"? I like to think that I would not have been satisfied and would have persisted, taking my question *why* right up to him. But then again, maybe I would have ended up as some denatured version of myself, content with whatever anodyne explanation was being handed out.

Certainly there were things other than atheism that distinguished my family, like our leaps-and-bounds upward mobility from the tenements of uptown Butte, Montana, to, by the time I became a teenager, the leafy exurbs of New England. My parents had eloped at the ages of eighteen and nineteen, bringing me into existence a decorous ten months or so later. At the time of my birth, my father was a copper miner in Butte, his father was a switchman for the Union Pacific, and my mother was cleaning boardinghouses. Thanks to a series of scholarships, my father made an almost unprecedented climb out of the mines, sweeping us along with him to Pittsburgh for graduate school in metallurgy, then through a series of white-collar jobs that took us to New York, Massachusetts, and finally Southern California, where we ran up against the irrefutable barrier of the Pacific Ocean and stopped right there.

Through all these moves—and there were enough so that I went to eleven different schools before entering college—Butte was our mythical touchstone and standard of authenticity. My parents had left when I was only two, but I treasured the summers when we got to return for a month or two, thanks to reductions in train ticket prices conferred by my paternal grandfather, the railroad switchman. I knew it was a hallowed place, and not only for the mountains. When anyone in the family did something heroic, criminal, or just plain self-destructive, my aunt Marcia would credit "the Butte in him [or her]." It wasn't a place, this Butte that lived on inside all its children, it was a condition of permanent defiance. All the generations of class struggle—miners' strikes, unexplained explosions, marches, and street brawls—boiled down to this, in my father and Marcia's exegesis: We don't take crap from anyone, never have and never will.

As a geographical place, Butte always takes a little explaining. Outsiders want to locate it in "Big Sky Country," where of course it is, and imagine it populated with cowboys, so I have to start by telling them that Butte was a city, a dense cosmopolitan city that had at its peak drawn sixty thousand people, mostly from Europe, to man its copper mines: Italy, Ireland, Wales, Serbo-Croatia, Bulgaria, Romania. In the Butte cemetery where my son and I went to lay wildflowers on the grave of IWW organizer Frank Little last summer, we found tombstones from the last century in Arabic, Cyrillic, and Chinese. There were Jews, too, probably from Russia—at least enough to form a minyan for the first synagogue ever built in Montana.

Butte people—"Butteans," you could call them, though I never heard anyone do so—did everything they could to distance themselves from the mythical cowboy-land of Montana, to the point of calling their city "Butte, USA." They even liked to extract it from the larger nation, quoting with pride the County Cork woman who saw her sons off from famine-ridden Ireland with the instruction, "Don't stop in America. Go straight on to Butte." Physically, Butte remains an anomaly: a cluster of multistory brick buildings, mostly empty now, and long-dead mining rigs jutting out from a mountainside like a quartz crystal sprouting out of a sheer rock face.

But today, in the shell that remains of postindustrial uptown Butte, there is no escaping the Big Sky anymore, no air pollution, for example, to shelter you from the all-encircling violence of the light. The other day I heard a Hidatsa man in Havre, Montana, struggling to answer an NPR interviewer who wanted to know what that "Big Sky" is like, and finally coming up with something about how it has "no edges," meaning, as I heard him, that it is everywhere and could swallow you up. You could be standing firmly on the ground, trusting in gravity to keep you earthbound, and then—poof—some part of you gets sucked up into the sky, leaving just a crisp of a person behind. This is what I always imagined must have happened to a cousin of my mother's, who lived on a farm in eastern Montana and out of the blue shot himself dead with a rifle when he was only nineteen. It was the blue, I guess, that got to him.

Copper had drawn people to Butte—the mine owners looking to get richer and the miners hoping to feed their children while their wives took in laundry. But when I went there on an achingly bright day last summer I formed a different impression—that Butte is where men went to escape from the sky. First they dug mines that ran a mile deep into the earth, which was about as far from the sky as you could get, and you had to be so desperate to get there that you'd risk being crushed in a collapsing tunnel or atomized in an explosion. Then they built the smelters to blur the sky with toxic smoke so that no miner emerging from the end of a shift would be exposed to the naked firmament, even for the short time it took him to get into the reassuring darkness of the bars, where you could count on the cigarette smoke to soften any stray intrusions of natural light. These are the lengths men will go to avoid being eaten alive by the emptiness, or at least that's how I began to see it as a child.

But I didn't know any history then and "class" was not available to me anyway as a category of analysis. No, the categories that shaped my childhood were much more primal than class or anything else, like gender, the sociologists have to offer. My childhood world was defined by desire and oppression, yearning and resistance, the push out and the shove back. You peek out and get poked in the eye; you reach out with your hand and it gets slapped down. So you try new angles for peeking and reaching, only to find new barriers thrown up in your way. You press against the wall, you jump to look over the top, you try crawling under until your knees are scraped and bloody.

If there was a recognizable demographic category in my childhood it was age. I entered the world as a child, of course, and I entered a world engaged in a war against children. We were the intruders; we could do nothing right; we were subject to constant rebuke. At home we were expected to work off our uselessness through chores—I was assigned, for example, to washing the dinner dishes at age six, when I had to stand on a chair to reach the sink, and when my brother was old enough, he dried. But we never did that task or any other well enough; dishes had to be rewashed, pots were not allowed to soak until the crust came off by itself. School was another site of correction. The penmanship was not neat enough, or I had neglected to carry a number while adding. Miss Sabatini, my third-grade teacher in Queens, made us sit with our hands crossed on our desks and our feet flat on the floor, all the time insisting that we "must learn self-control." Although clearly if we had any real measure of control over ourselves and our lives we would be out in the playground, running and screaming.

In this war against children we all enter on the losing side and carry our wounds along to the next generation. My mother had been abandoned as a small child to her maternal grandparents, ostensibly because her parents couldn't afford her, which may have been true at the time, because her father was drinking so heavily, in the normal way of miners, that her mother had had to humiliate herself by going to the shift boss at the mine and asking him for help, requesting that he give her the paychecks directly. But my mother's parents did manage to raise their two younger children on their own, no problem, while my mother, the unwanted one, suffocated in the Victorian prison of her grandmother's house in Nelson, British Columbia, which was devoted to the display of precious teacups and silver spoons commemorating important events in Canadian history. Maybe, in defense of my maternal grandparents, the reason they didn't take my mother back even when they had the means to do so was that she was supposed to function as a replacement child for the daughter (who would have grown up to be my mother's aunt) my great-grandparents had lost at any early age to some routine early-twentieth-century infectious disease. My mother's job was to drive the sadness out of that house in Nelson, but I suspect the sadness won.

According to my mother, there had been a similar deficit in my father's past. He worshipped his mother, whom I remember as an obese, perpetually sedentary woman with stringy hair pulled back in a bun. But his mother had eyes—and what eyes, so fascinatingly deep-set and blue!—only for her eldest son, Gordon, who was by reputation in Butte not only a drunkard, brawler, and fornicator, but a murderer too. (He was not the only man on my paternal side who was said to have killed another man. Murder was apparently not such a serious crime in Butte.) Uncle Gordon, a railroad worker like his father, was crushed under his own train at the age of thirty, either pushed or falling-down drunk. But nothing my father achieved—his degrees and eventually, by working-class Butte standards, his wealth—ever threatened Gordon's primacy in his mother's heart.

The loathsomeness and dependency of children seemed to drag down the entire adult female sex; at least that was the impression I formed from the vantage point of my own family, My mother's anger was the central force field in our home, its targets divided between my father, who got to leave every morning and often delayed his return till late at night, and me. She cleaned and scrubbed and seethed and cursed, to what I saw early on was an unusual degree, since my playmates judged her to be "mean." When in an outbreak of defiance I passed this information on to her, along with a personal declaration of hatred, she washed my mouth out with soap.

Home, in those earliest years, was a standoff between my

mother's dreams of middle-class orderliness and the routine chaos of life. When we lived in Pittsburgh I shared a tiny bedroom with my little brother where I once woke up to find him painting the wall with shit mined from his diaper. One bedroom—there must have been three total—was occupied by a married couple we took in as boarders, whose nightly fights—or, as my mother suggested by saying, "Some people enjoy that kind of thing," sadomasochistic rituals—shook the house. When I was about twelve, at least old enough to have sprouted the first appalling pubic hairs, I slept on a fold-out coach in the "den" in our house in Waltham, Massachusetts. To get to the bathroom I had to pass through the living room, where at night my mother would be alone, ironing and working herself into rage at my father's perpetual absence. Once, I was too terrified to get up and walk by her for a second time and resorted to wetting the bed. When I gave up on sleep and confessed, she slapped me hard before allowing me to change the sheet.

My first efforts at systematic observation of a scientific or at least naturalist sort took place at home, in an effort to understand and predict my parents' behavior. My mother's alternations between "nice" and "mean," for example—did these follow a predictable pattern, in which, for example, a "nice" day, in which she might peaceably instruct me in cooking or sewing, would be inevitably followed by a day of curses, slaps, and, on my part, tears? Then there was the mystery of alcohol and its effects. My father had been a heavy drinker since adolescence, or so my maternal grandmother told me much later. She did not like to say anything bad about him or any of her children's spouses, nor did she like to confide much in anyone, this quiet, stoic woman who had abandoned her first child, but she did blame my father for spreading his alcoholism to my mother, where it had begun to have a visibly deleterious effect by the time I was eight. It was then that they had their first drunk-driving accident serious enough to draw blood, coming home way after midnight (I was the babysitter), lurching, cursing, and bleeding from their faces. In my observation, alcohol changed a person by removing their customary mask, so that some "true self," or so I thought, characterized by unconstrained anger and contempt, showed forth. The effect of the accident, though, was to leave their faces permanently altered by scars so that their "true selves" bore the label "damaged."

Compared to home, school was spacious, austere, and well lit. At first I hated it, and routinely vomited in the morning before setting out—not deliberately, but out of fear. Fear of the teachers and, although it's hard to admit this now, fear also of being separated from my mother, whose dark energy, after all, was the reigning force in my life, like weather, only occurring mostly indoors. I had two recurrent nightmares as a child: In one of them, I would be walking home from school the usual way but unable to find my home. Everything else on our block would be the same, but the building that we lived in would be gone without a trace. In the other one, I was being chased by lions and there never had been any home. There were good dreams too, and in them I had the ability to fly.

It wasn't until about fourth grade that I discovered a reason to achieve in school: By doing so, I could win my father's praise. Not that that was an unmixed benefit, because the more I rose in his esteem, the more I earned my mother's wrath. Those were the sides that shaped up in our family—him and me versus my mother and to a lesser extent my brother and sister. My mother valued education, not having gotten beyond high school herself, and read novels whenever she wasn't cooking or cleaning, pausing now and then to fill me in on the plot, but the family factions overshadowed our shared allegiance to books. To the extent that I was my

father's favorite, I was his proxy and her enemy. She never discouraged me from studying, but neither did she ever allow me to forget
what I was—a child and, worse, a girl. "You think you're so above
it all," she would say, referring to my shortcomings in the house-
cleaning department. But the "it" I was attempting to rise above
would catch up with me. Just wait and see; I would end up like
her. If I was lucky, that is, for it was unlikely that anyone as sullen,
as withdrawn and negligent about personal appearance as I was
would ever find a man.

But if you are thinking this is the usual story of dysfunction and
abuse, then I'm doing a poor job of telling it, and projecting my
own standards as a parent onto a time, and a class, when children
were still regarded as miscreants rather than the artisanal projects
that they have become today. It's not easy to explain my parents'
complicated role in repressing and inspiring me, clamping down
and letting go. Who am I, a former child, to tell the stories of these
giants of the earth, whose ambitions propelled us from one city
or state to another, bound to each other in our constant motion?
They were driven by their own yearnings, in part, for the usual
status and money things—a car, eventually the larger homes and
second car—all the stuff my mother would eventually renounce
as "empty materialism." Who can blame them, when you bear in
mind what they came from? By the time I was twelve, they were
beginning to acquire some of the objects that seemed talismanic
of a broader perspective than what had been available to them
in Butte—framed Audubon prints on the wall, the *Ladies' Home
Journal* and *Life* magazines on the coffee table, new furniture as
opposed to used. But their yearnings went further, toward some
unspecified "more," some great challenge or adventure. They were
rebels too, and I respected that, even as I rebelled against them.

Ah, hell. Even now, insulated by so many intervening years, I could choke on the pity of it. They started out so young and brave, my parents, and ended up such sordid messes. Only one thing saved my father from dying as a slobbering drunk, and that was Alzheimer's disease, alcohol being unavailable in the nursing home he finally expired in. As for my mother, she didn't live long enough to find out that I grew up to have all the things she craved, that the entire package, plus some, would be delivered exactly a generation late—the adventure, the causes, the friends and hot romances. She died, too, before we could settle things between us, on her third suicide attempt. The earlier ones had led to successful stomach-pumpings, but in the last one she managed to down enough pills before anyone noticed the cessation of vital signs.

We will get back to my father soon enough, that great man-god and Shiva-like genius of self-destruction. It was he, after all, who instructed me to always ask *why*, and thereby started, or at least abetted, the entire project. But we are still in prehistory here, before the situation was clearly defined and the question formulated, before I was even much of a reader, when I was driven largely by the desire to explore, to get outdoors and see new places. All I required was a hill to climb, a corner to turn, a shore to run along. In Pittsburgh my wanderings were confined to the grassless enclosure made by our row houses, where all the children played, but things opened up with our move to Queens, where—this was a long time ago—there were still vacant lots grown over with trees and streets that ended in mystery. Better yet were two of the places we lived in in Massachusetts, Waltham and Hamilton, which offered woods and meadows and streams. Before I explored books and libraries, I explored with my body—pushing it up rocks or trees, hurling it through space on my bicycle. This is what I wanted before I wanted answers; I wanted to move and run and climb.

Every kid wants these things, but mine was perhaps an especially acute case of what Edward Wilson calls "biophilia." Part of it may have been the sheer lack of alternative sites for exploration. We had no malls then, only department stores, and these had little to offer me, since the clothes my mother did not sew were ordered from the Sears catalog. Besides, the man-made environment, at least in its emerging proto-suburban form, was too numbingly repetitive—each brick or shingle designed to be exactly like any other. Nature, in contrast, excels in the art of small differences. No two branches or clouds or waves in the ocean are the same; each commands our close attention.

In fact I came to hate the built environment, both for its dullness and the way it shut me out. When a house came up on what had been a vacant lot, which was happening all the time then in Queens, that lot was barred to me, just as the common fields were barred to my British ancestors by the enclosures in the eighteenth and nineteenth centuries. The first "political" act of my life would now be categorized as ecoterrorism: I recruited another eight-year-old to help me vandalize a "model home" in a new development a block from where my family lived. We broke into the house on a weekday after five, when the realtors weren't around, ripped up their papers, smashed windows, and defaced the clean-painted walls with hurled ink. For months I lived in fear of being caught, because I understood that the defense of trees and empty lots was worse than mischief; it was a crime.

There were no limits on my outdoor life, especially after my father taught me to ride a bike—a skill I came to value almost as much as reading. In my physical explorations, as in reading, family dysfunction served me well; just as my mother's rage pushed me into books, her indifference—one might say neglect—left me without any outdoor limits. She made a point of not confining us, saying that she had been smothered by her overprotective grandparents,

and that there would be none of that for her own children—no distances too far to go, no neighborhoods labeled as dangerous, no
time of night too late. My father was equally indifferent to physical danger. He was an athletic guy—a competitive ski jumper at
Butte High—who trusted his strength even after years of lab and
desk work had sabotaged his upper body. Once, when we lived in
Queens, he took us out into the East River in a rented rowboat,
where the sky turned gray and the wind and currents drove us ever
farther out into the bay. We had no life jackets, nor could anyone of
us except my father really swim, and although he became unnaturally silent and concentrated, I could detect no worry in his face.

Sometime in the late fifties, a hurricane struck us in Massachusetts, in Hamilton, where we were truly out in the country,
surrounded by pines and elms. My father was at work, leaving
my mother, brother, and sister and me to run from window to
window watching the trees crash down around the house. I, naturally, wanted to go outdoors and run around and test my strength
against the storm, and my mother said okay. If you ever needed
evidence of her unfitness as a parent, this was it. Why did she let
us go out—my brother, who was probably eight or less, and me?
Maybe she thought, with the power out and the trees falling, that
it was the end of the world anyway and we might as well participate firsthand. Or maybe we were having some rare moment of
mother-daughter concordance in which she could see as well as I
that there was freedom in the storm for anyone willing to go outside and exult in it.

So my brother and I slanted our bodies against the hundred-
mile-per-hour wind and headed down to the bridge, about a quar-
ter mile away. He fell behind, and when a tree snapped down
between the two of us I looked back and to my surprise saw his
face open into helpless bawling. He couldn't see me because I had

crouched down beside a stone wall, and he must have thought that I had been crushed by the falling tree. Even at that moment, I had no idea of danger. The amazing thing was that my brother, with whom I was so often locked in trivial combat, loved me enough to cry.

I didn't think much about the future when I was a child—who does? The future self is different, with aims and desires unknowable in one's current form. Besides, I had no control over it. We might move arbitrarily at any time, plunging me from multiplication into long division or, much later, from solid geometry into trigonometry, leaving me scrambling to keep afloat. But to the extent that I did imagine a future, it held an ever-widening range for my explorations—more hills and valleys, shorelines and dunes. I would be a lawyer, or so I thought for a few weeks after reading a biography of Clarence Darrow, or a scientist, as suggested by a biography of Marie Curie, but mostly I would learn to drive, acquire a car, and penetrate huge new vistas by myself.

The idea that there might be a limit to my explorations, a natural cutoff in the form of death, was slow to dawn on me. Without that, though, there could have been no "situation" demanding explanations. Yes, I lost pets with sickening regularity—my crippled German shepherd Caesar run over on the street, a kitten crushed under my father's tire—but the humans around me seemed durable enough, despite my nighttime fears that my parents would be claimed by their final DUI and never make it home. Mostly, I encountered death in books, where it largely functioned as a plot turn or finale: Beth died in *Little Women*, Roland in his *Chanson*, Achilles in *The Iliad*, and their deaths were grand and necessary.

I read all my parents' books, with few restrictions. The censored items included Kinsey's book on male sexuality, which I skimmed through without enlightenment, and—also banned for sexual content—Mika Waltari's novel *The Egyptian*, which I read anyway.

The censors should have paid more attention to their copy of Bulfinch's *Age of Fable or Beauties of Mythology*, which I read over and over, and not only for the juicy intrigues of the gods. In it I learned—mostly from the Norse and ancient Greeks—that we are mortal and that heroes have chafed against this condition from the dawn of time. Even more instructive was the *Rubaiyat of Omar Khayyam*, which my parents possessed in a beautifully illustrated edition. Who were these Persians? I had no idea, but when Khayyam said, "Ah, Wilderness were Paradise enow!" he spoke for me, even with that crazy Old English word for "enough." So I struggled to absorb the bad news too, delivered in one elegant quatrain after another, that this life is "like Snow upon the Desert's dusty Face, lighting a little hour or two…"

The full sorriness of it didn't hit me until my maternal grandfather let slip the fact that death was not only empty and inglorious, but approaching at breakneck pace. I didn't get to know my mother's father well; like most of the older men in my family, he was a man of few words, and those doled out only grudgingly. His wife, my grandmother, told me that he had been a dazzling wit as a young man, like my brilliant aunt Jean, and that that's what drew her to him. There were rumors, encouraged maliciously by my own father and given some credence by Granddad's high cheekbones and aquiline nose, that he was a Native American or partly so, but the official story is that he was white and born to the Simmons family, small farmers in Montana's eastern plains. After his mother died in childbirth, he and his siblings were dispersed to other families, which is how he acquired the surname Oxley. He ran away from the Oxleys, though, who had been using him like an indentured servant, and spent his teenage years living among the Kootenai people, learning to fish and track and hunt. Inevitably, like any other male of his class, he ended up in the mines in Butte, where, after overcoming the drinking problem mentioned earlier, he rose in middle age to the estimable position of shift boss. He smoked Raleighs, for the coupons, and fished whenever he could, though he never took me with him.

We were standing in his garden one summer morning, where he was showing me his prizewinning hollyhocks and sweet peas, when—apropos of what I do not know—he said, "It all goes by so fast." Something like that anyway, about how you think you have all this time, and then it all runs out. In his case, at this moment, he was right. He had retired from the mines about a year earlier and would die of a heart attack within another year or two—meaning that in his adult life not much more than a couple of years were spent continuously above ground, in the wind and the possibility of sunlight. He was dying right in front of me, in other words, a once strong and vital man, left old and baffled within the transient carnival of flowers, and only the hills, gray and ruined by Butte's smelters, would keep on going as they were.

No doubt I asked my parents about death, and no doubt they answered conscientiously. This was one of my mother's greatest virtues—she said we could ask her anything, and unless the question touched on sex or reproduction, when you would get some gobbledygook about ovaries and fallopian tubes, without the slightest reference to actual humans, the answers usually made some sense. I can't recall a specific conversation on the subject of death, but I know exactly what the response would have been: There is no afterlife; we are here and then we're gone. Death is a fact; get used to it. And why are you just standing around with nothing to do?

What no one could explain was how the fact of death applied to me. To accept death was to believe in, or otherwise vividly imagine, a world without me in it. But *believing* anything was exactly what a "realist" should refuse to do. I had no evidence for the continuation of the world without me. How could I? So if death stalked the world, cutting down kittens and heroes alike, there was still no reason to think it would come for me.

Then, just a few months shy of my thirteenth birthday, came the onset of menstruation and with it the realization that I too was marked for personal destruction. I didn't want to grow up, which I understood as a defection to the enemy side, and resisted—unsuccessfully—the pressure to start setting my hair every night and applying a smear of pink lipstick before leaving the house. What was the meaning of that lipstick anyway—that I had tasted the cotton candy and was ready to proceed as directed? Some of my mother's interventions were welcome insofar as they helped mitigate the damage of puberty, like the ointments for acne and the first padded starter bra. But mostly I saw her efforts to induct me into adulthood much as a calf might see its mother's explanations of veal: I was being recruited into the great death march of biology—be born, reproduce, die.

I resolved that one thing would distinguish me from the long line of those who had fallen before me, the great-great-grandparents and so on stretching back to Ireland and Scotland and before that the Eurasian plains the Celts had originally come streaming out of: Surely they had also grasped "the situation," but I was going to find out *why*, which I understood even at the time to be a protest as well as a question. What my grandfather was trying to warn me about was that there would be an end to exploration—over that last hill or bend in the trail—a bracket or final punctuation mark awaiting me, and that the end wouldn't necessarily come when I had finished my heroic mission, as in the case of Roland or Achilles. It could come in the middle of things, before I'd gotten any traction. Which meant that for me, still a child of not quite thirteen, time was already running out.

CHAPTER 2

Typing Practice

I didn't start my journal with the idea of recording my progress toward the ultimate truth. I was nowhere near bombastic enough to think I had anything important to say, even to my future self. It had begun, modestly enough, as typing practice, undertaken to avoid taking a typing course required for all ninth-grade girls. In my experience, any class or assembly restricted to girls was going to be in some way degrading, like the one where we'd been convened to receive the information that from now on our bodies would be producing poisons that would need to be discharged on a monthly basis, through an unspecified orifice. The restriction of the typing requirement to girls suggested some sort of connection between our festering genitals and the need to serve in a clerical-type occupation, perhaps as a punishment. So it would be safer, I figured, to learn typing on my own, without the supervision of some middle-aged woman who had long since been defeated by the buildup of toxins. But what to type? "I'm beginning to dread these original typing practices," I wrote about a month into them, a bit melodramatically, because no one was exactly forcing me. "I guess the trick is to write what I think as I think it and not worry about how it sounds."

Most of the first, unpremeditated entries are desultory accounts of my first summer in Lowell, where I had few friends and no escape from the built environment unless my mother could be badgered into driving us to the beach. Aesthetically, Lowell was a tragic demotion for me—from the open spaces of Hamilton to the blocks of empty brick mills, from the frothy little Ipswich River, which a kid could almost navigate on a raft, to the dark, tired, overworked Merrimack. But Lowell had one big thing going for it—the public library, the same one, it turns out, that had been used by young Jack Kerouac just a few decades before me, where, as he wrote in one of his early novels, he'd "become interested in old classical looking library books, some of them falling apart and from the darkest shelf in the Lowell Public Library, found there by me in my overshoes at closing time."

Those that did not actually fall apart in his hands probably ended up in mine, because the journal from this period is full of brief, embarrassing reports on what I was reading—*Tender Is the Night*, for example, which I found "confusing" and "improbable" since it was about "the love of an 18 year old girl for a 30-ish man who is already married and in love with his wife etc." In a similarly dimwitted way, I judged an Agatha Christie mystery to be "very exciting with an excellent plot and interesting characters." And what are we to make of this entry, which comes immediately after some gushing about the beauty and mystery of cellular mitosis, which I had also found out about in the library?

Another interesting scientific item was in the Scientific American. Namely the article on the discovery of the antiproton. The speculation concerning the meaning of this discovery was not news to me at all tho and came nowhere near my spectacular ideas in imaginativeness.

Yes, I was blown away by the discovery of antimatter, but did I actually think that the commentary in *Scientific American* should be judged by its "imaginativeness"? And what were my "spectacular ideas" about physics, which are not explained in the journal? The early entries are adolescent in the full derogatory sense of the word. Or to put it more kindly: A lot happens in fifty years. You learn to spell better; you would never commit a solecism like "unrevocably," which shows up in my very first journal entry. Your writing becomes less stilted, so there is no way, for example, that you would compose the sentence, "I have lately been considering the utter futility of the lives of almost every living thing," which is also from that first entry. More importantly, you would have learned to shut up about the "utter futility" and, as we like to say now, get on with your life. It's normal to disavow your teenage self, otherwise how could we "grow"? Certainly in the 1950s, when I hit my teens, the "central developmental task" that psychologists had devised for this phase in the lives of young humans was gradually to put away existential angst and unrealistic ambitions for the benumbed state known as "maturity."

After a couple of weeks, on about the fifth entry, I abandoned my original rationale for writing and switched without comment to longhand. Typing could wait. I had discovered that writing—with whatever instrument—was a powerful aid to thinking, and thinking was what I now resolved to do. You can think without writing, of course, as most people do and have done throughout history, but if you can condense today's thought into a few symbols preserved on a surface of some kind—paper or silicon—you don't have to rethink it tomorrow. You can even give it a name like "yesterday's thought" or "the meaning of life" and carry it along in your pocket like a token that can be traded in for ever greater abstractions. The reason I eventually became a writer is that writing makes thinking easier, and even as a verbally underdeveloped fourteen-year-old I knew that if I wanted to understand "the situation," thinking was what I had to do.

I got the idea from my father; at least he was the most insistent about it. What do you do when confronted with an inexplicable and alarming situation? Well, you can panic or give in to some other tyrannical emotion, like dread. Or you can escape into a book or a puzzle or, judging from the adults around me, a bottle of gin. But there is another possible response to the unknown and potentially menacing, and that is *thinking*. I suspect my father first came across it as a child, because he was exceptionally good at it, and it can be one of those little things, like being able to wiggle your ears, that gets you attention in a group. He had a photographic memory, among other superhuman capacities, and even the blurry version of it that I inherited was enough to make me stand out in games like "movie star" that I played with other kids on my grandparents' block in Butte. The idea was to see who could list the most names in that category, and although I had seen hardly any movies outside of the Disney genre, I could keep producing candidates—Tyrone Power, Elizabeth Taylor—long after the other kids had exhausted their cinematic memories. No doubt my father could perform similar or much better tricks as a child, and maybe these helped him hold his own against the big boys, especially his brothers.

If he wasn't already an experienced thinker, he would certainly have had to become one in the mines. You may think of mining as the application of brute muscle to mountains and rock—and it is that too, of course. Long after he had left the mines for laboratories and eventually offices, the mining experience was still recorded in the muscles of his back and etched into his left arm as a blue skull and crossbones tattoo, a dermatological remnant, as I saw it, of the rough world we had left behind in Butte, where death was not to be flinched at and sometimes even sought out. But mining is also an intellectual exercise, requiring the combined skills of a plumber, a carpenter, and an electrician as well as an explosives expert. You had to be able to judge the load strength of a beam or the friability of rock at a glance and do instant calculations in your head, because one false step or misplaced stick of dynamite could blow you into body parts or at least send a few digits flying off on their own. So this was the mental procedure, which even a little girl could learn: First, size up the situation. Make sure you have all the facts, and nothing but the facts—no folklore, no conventional wisdom, no lazy assumptions. Then examine the facts for patterns and connections. Make a prediction. See if it works. And if it doesn't work, start all over again.

This, in the most rudimentary sense, is what science is about, and it was science that saved my father from the mines. He won a scholarship, possibly from the Anaconda Copper Mining Company itself, to attend the Butte School of Mines during the day, while continuing to work in the mines at night. There was no question of studying literature or astronomy in Butte; all the school had to offer was metallurgy and mining-related technology. Within metallurgy, what intrigued him was the crystal structure of minerals, the way the atoms stack up to form a tight-knit community, so intricately and multiply bonded to each other that the whole is almost impenetrable to a pick or other cutting device. I think he wanted to know what he was up against there in the mines—what it was that accounted for the hardness of matter and the difficulty of turning rocks into usable ore. On a good day, he would go through his mineral collection with me, pointing out the scaliness of mica, the greenish hue of copper-based rocks, the redness of iron oxides. Or he would bring home specimens from the lab, some benign, like a little chunk of bright yellow sulfur in a vial, and some not so benign, like a ball of liquid mercury I could roll around in my hand, blithely unaware of its toxicity. The lesson of all this was that every visible, palpable object, every rock or grain of sand, is a clue in the larger mystery of how the universe is organized and put together—a mystery that it was our job, as thinking beings, to solve. I was flattered to be included in this enterprise, but always on guard lest one dumb question or halting answer elicit a burst of biting contempt.

For me, never having had to swing a pick at a wall of rock or anything else, the original lure of thinking was only in part as a tool for problem-solving. The main thing was that it beat the alternatives—panic, for example, and terror. Way before puberty, before the journal, before the formulation of my life's mission, when I must have been eight or younger, I had a rule: "Think in complete sentences." No giving way to inner screams or sobs— just keep stringing out words in grammatical order. This was a way to keep from going under when the waters were rising, for example, on one of those pale winter Sunday afternoons that my father spent "resting" on the couch, drinking until the rest deepened into what we euphemized as sleep. Then my mother, who had absorbed the novel idea of "companionate marriage" from the women's magazines, would start looking for a fight with anyone who was around and sentient. If I attempted to rebut her accusations or evade her demands—"but I did the dishes this morning" or "he hit me first"—I would then be liable to the charge of "sassing," which was a speech crime punishable by slapping and invective, as in "you goddamned little brat." It was at times like this that the complete-sentences rule proved its usefulness, so long as the sentences were silent.

You can think of it this way: Thought is electrical activity—a bunch of neurons firing up and connecting to each other—but all this mental circuitry has to function in a liquid environment that swarms with hormones and other small molecules whose levels can register in the mind as emotions. When the liquid starts turning into tar—or worse, going into whirlpool mode and threatening total disintegration—the only way out is to strengthen the neuronal scaffolding and try to keep the circuits dry. From "think in complete sentences" the rule evolved into "think."

So I would get to the answers by thinking—not by dreaming or imagining and of course not by praying or pleading to imaginary others. "The situation" would yield to sheer force of mind. As I wrote to myself, I had decided on "an orderly plan of attack, systematic, geometrical." If A, then B, and so forth. I was so confident that this method would work that when I raised the question of how we "can live happily knowing or thinking that our existence as individuals is so brief and futile," I could go on to promise in the same journal entry that "I shall try and write the answer to that question when my present ideas are straightened out."

The first problem was to identify the minimum of bare, incontestable facts that any philosophical inquiry has to begin with, and this brought me up immediately against the problem of the reliability of other people. Did they have anything useful to say, anything that could be built upon? All in all, school was not proving to be a reliable source of information. There was, for example, the science teacher who drew his biology lessons from the book of Genesis and exhibited a sneering contempt for anyone who imagined that rocks had been around for more than six thousand years. I entertained myself in his class by concentrating on developing an empathic relationship with the trash can that sat between his desk and my seat. It was gray and squat and humble, not a cylinder but a slice of a cone, hinting at the existence of an invisible person or people whose job was to empty it every night. Just as I could intuit the subjective state of every person I encountered, there was nothing to stop me from imagining that, in their own way, even objects were alive. What did it feel like, assuming that a trash can could feel, to be a receptacle for every bit of garbage that came your way? Did it choke on each piece of refuse that came flying into it, or did it take an austere pride in its silent self-abnegation?

Or I might mention the eighth-grade English teacher who kept me after class to accuse me of plagiarizing my paper on *The Iliad*, since it was obviously something I could not have written myself. Perhaps in an attempt to make me feel the wrath of Achilles pounding in my temples, right then and there, she announced that my grade for the paper would be F. Also in the eighth grade, Mr. Cummings, the kindly martinet who served as principal—or as he liked to put it, headmaster—of Moody Junior High School in Lowell, intercepted me in the corridor one day to inform me gravely that my IQ, so stellar a year ago, had taken a sudden dive. This was not surprising to me, given the other mutilations being inflicted by puberty. If my body was going to get all leaky and mossy, why not my mind? Although it occurred to me after a few days of reflection that the real sign of mental deterioration was that I had allowed myself to be dismayed even briefly by the news, because it was not my intelligence but the very idea of "IQ" that had been discredited by the latest test result.

Math, which had been a source of consolation when the subject was geometry or algebra, offered a fresh reason for wariness when the topic turned to imaginary numbers. *Imaginary* numbers? How could anyone introduce the concept with a straight face? Would a history teacher who'd been lecturing about generals and kings suddenly announce that the next topic would be pixies and elves? As it happened, I already knew about these odd creatures, probably from the science writer Isaac Asimov, and knew that they were an affront to human reason. Think about it: Imaginary numbers are defined as multiples of the square root of −1, but there can be no number corresponding to the "square root of −1," because if you multiply −1 by −1, you get, of course, +1, which is why Descartes in the seventeenth century had derided them as "imaginary" and refused to accept their existence. And who could be more respectable than Descartes, the discoverer, or so it seemed, of the "Cartesian plane"—that infinite flatland on which abstract equations took physical form as lines and curves, soaring and diving across the paper like living creatures?

But for my teacher, a dowdy white-haired woman whose tired eyes suggested she went home by bus to an even more elderly mother, it was just another day at the blackboard, without the slightest threat of paradox. So I raised my hand, more or less as a public service, and pointed out the absurdity of "the square root of −1," at least relative to everything we had learned so far in math. She blinked, I'll say that, but just barely—acknowledging that it was an interesting point and moving right along. At least I had tried to warn my classmates, not that any of them appeared to be listening. If you accept imaginary numbers without raising a question, you'll swallow any goddamn thing they decide to stuff down your throat.

I wanted to believe, and perhaps had believed when I was younger, that my parents were trustworthy sources. They both read copiously, after all, and liked to argue, discuss, and point out the multiple failings of the people outside our family, a dangerously high proportion of whom they classified as zombies, cult members, or morons coasting along on their sinecures. There were the young nuns, for example, novitiates actually, whom I walked past every morning on my way to school—girls not much older than myself wearing long gray habits, eyes downcast as they marched up the hill in chain gang formation, to what dark ritual I do not know. If there hadn't been so many of them, and if they hadn't been followed by two huge mothlike grown-up nuns, I might have attempted a conversation or at least a nod, but I never even suc- ceeded in making eye contact. I just walked on by, thanking God or fate or whatever spirits arrange these things, for giving me the parents I had, who, whatever their faults, which were legion, would never think of offering a child up to God.

But could they be trusted, these rationalist, atheist parents of mine? You might think my father would have been a touchstone of truthfulness, with his insistence on logic, on always probing further with the question *why*, but on small matters he was a ha- bitual liar, as we were reminded almost every day. My mother put great effort into the production of dinner, which typically fea- tured meat, gravy, potatoes, and a home-baked dessert, like the butterscotch cream pie my father craved—everything cooked soft because his teeth were so bad. The food would be getting cold on the plates when he'd call to say he'd been caught up in a meet- ing, or maybe he didn't call at all, and we kids ate alone while our mother fumed and lit one cigarette after another. We all knew the "meetings" took place in bars or possibly motel rooms, because he came back, if he came back early enough for me to still be awake, in a loose-lipped, goofy frame of mind, smelling of liquor. I don't think he would lie about something like the specific gravity of mercury or the boiling point of water, unless, of course, it was the only way to win an argument against someone who was equally tipsy.

As for my mother, I had once trusted her enough to try to enlist her help with my quest, because she was after all a major source of information, an insatiable consumer of novels and magazines with no other regular confidante than myself. For months I had been observing adult behavior, meaning mostly my parents', and decided it could be sorted into two categories. There were the things that they did primarily to promote their own survival, like eating, and there were the things they did for the sake of biological reproduction, a category that included putting on makeup and cooking for their children. If they were doing anything else with their time—like writing poetry or attempting to contact extraterrestrial beings—it was not in evidence to me. Just carry on those germ cells and populate the earth; that seemed to be the entire agenda.

I saw this as a remarkable simplification, almost a theoretical breakthrough. When I approached her with it, my mother was washing her nylons in the bathroom sink, which I recognized as another reproductive-type duty. Could this be all there is, I asked her—just trying to prolong our own lives while reproducing the species? And what was the point?

There are a lot of things she could have said then, if she'd had the confidence, if she'd straightened up from the sink and taken a deep breath, because certainly she'd read enough to know what the liberal, secular answers might be. She could have said, no, we are not just your run-of-the-mill terrestrial animals. You don't have to be religious to see that we also live for love or, I don't know, some other sentimental abstraction like beauty or justice or truth. But she didn't even try to answer, just glared at me with that familiar combination of resentment and disgust, and then asked why I had nothing to do. It was many years before I realized that the question had been a grave personal insult, an attack on what she must have felt was the triviality of her own existence.

By the time we lived in Lowell she didn't hit me so much anymore, for the simple reason that I was getting to be taller than she was—in other words, more of a reach. This had to have been a challenging adjustment for her, just as my brother's growing strength would pose a problem for my father in a couple of years. Too bad for any parent who has become accustomed to ruling by force, because at some point the kids just get too big to slap around. Then new and subtler weapons have to be brought into play, such as insults and invasions of privacy, like the time I came home from school to find my drawers emptied onto the bedroom floor because she had peeked into them and found them unacceptably messy. I could have cried, and probably did just a little, although I knew this would make my eyes sting through the hours of homework and reading ahead. I picked my clothes up off the floor and put them away, but to this day I've never understood why the clothes you're not wearing have to be hidden, and why, if you're going to go to the trouble of hiding them, you have to first fold them in some precisely specified way.

But my mother's worst, to this day most unforgivable crime was to accuse me of harboring incestuous designs on my father. I don't remember what brought this on, if I even knew at the time. She didn't use the word "incest," which I probably wouldn't have known anyway, nor of course did she offer any kind of evidence. She just announced as a scientific fact—"Freud said"—that girls are "sexually attracted" to their fathers, which is obviously why I favored my father over her. I managed to keep my face aligned in a disciplined expression of scorn and indifference, even as I crumpled inside. So every glorious moment in which I had said something that made my father laugh or at least snicker, every instance in which he'd taken the time to explain some natural phenomenon to me—all these were now revealed as evidence of a hideous perversity.

I didn't write about this accusation in my journal, which was reserved for loftier matters; I didn't even have a category under which to file it in my brain. Sexual desire for a man—or for anyone or anything? Sex was something that occasionally happened to women in novels, generally leading to poverty or death. I had read about sexual desire in psychology books from the library, where it was sternly represented as a "drive," which seemed to involve being propelled by whips, and I occasionally received mysterious bulletins from unexplored parts of my body. My mother had warned me often enough about this drive, which is what she blamed for—or credited with—her transformation from a teenager into a housewife, and no doubt the same thing had undone my cousin Patsy Jane, one of my childhood companions in Butte, who was only two years older than me and already a mother. Apparently there was no honorable way out, because if you frustrate the sex urge, all you get is depravity, as my mother illustrated with the story she had read somewhere about a nun who repeatedly stuck a pencil into her vagina in order to warrant medical attention to the afflicted area.

As for the sex act itself—and recall that at this time sex was still an "act" known as intercourse—I had recently received some disturbing information from my best friend in Lowell, Bernice, who had a cousin who claimed to have observed her parents performing it. Bernice was Greek Orthodox, so we spent a great deal of time arguing about religion, but we generally faced the indignities of adolescence, like "monthlies" and the pressure to "develop," as a united front. We were walking to school when she asked me if I wanted to know what her cousin had seen, and with some trepidation I told her I did. The words didn't come easily to her because they weren't the kind of words we ever had occasion to use. I kept on walking, trying to be cool about it, but she might as well have told me that the participants sprout horns out of their belly buttons and proceed to gore each other. It was beyond ludicrous. I said something intemperate involving "Jesus," or maybe all the way to "Jesus Christ," leading her to scold me for taking the Lord's name in vain. But she knew as well as I did that the real horror lay elsewhere, in what *she* had just said. If this was what adults dressed up and put on makeup for, flirted and schemed for, even saw as a defining activity of their lives, then why had they been put in charge?

Somewhere around this time I stopped listening to my mother if I could avoid it, even in her gabby, confiding moods when she went on about books she was reading or the stupidity of the people she'd been forced to socialize with the night before. I noted in my journal that "she thinks I am cold and withdrawn," which was exactly the effect I was striving for. She went on, on more than one occasion, to warn me that my "coldness" would make me permanently unattractive to men, meaning that I was, generally speaking, unworthy of love. But still I didn't hate her, even for the accusation of illicit Freudian yearnings, because I understood that no one could have lobbed such a stinging wad of shame out into the world without having a considerable personal reserve of it to draw on.

I'd still like to know what she had against me. Was I a scapegoat for my father? Or possibly for my aunt Jean? Or was I some voodoo amalgam of both of them—people who were more self-confident than she was, quicker and funnier? The problem with families is not that you get stuck in the same persona for life, which is what everyone complains about, but that you're always getting confused with someone else and end up taking the blame for them. You may think of yourself as a freestanding individual, a unique point of consciousness in the universe, but in many ways you are just subbing for absent family members or departed ancestors. You may even literally change places with them, like the night that first year in Lowell when I heard my mother calling for me from her bedroom, where I found her lying on the floor drunk, wearing only her panties and whimpering that she couldn't get up. My father was asleep or passed out, so I had to turn into the mother—or at least the motherlike figure in this sordid drama—and haul her to the toilet like a big floppy baby.

Or possibly she didn't dislike me in particular at all and had just absorbed the Freudian propaganda, so readily available in the middlebrow culture then, that little children are all hell-bent on fucking their parents. She had informed me once that my father had an unwholesome attachment to his own mother, and that this somehow explained his shortcomings as a husband, his failure to form a mature and responsible bond. In her version of Freudianism, the human world was fraught with illicit intergenerational longings—between her daughter and her husband, her husband and his mother—all of them bypassing her.

Contrary to her lurid imaginings, puberty had also driven a wedge between my father and me. Up till that point he might have imagined me as some sort of successor to him—a scientist of course, since that's what "smart" people did—though I was not as smart as he was, nor could anyone hope to be, given that he claimed an IQ of 187, which put the rest of us at the level of insects by comparison. Still, he had always allowed that I was perhaps just capable of growing up to make a scientific discovery that would lead to some modest improvement in human life, a cure for acne being his usual example of a breakthrough that I might aspire to. But now that I was fourteen, it was getting hard to deny that I was on course to turn into a woman, and a woman couldn't be a scientist without being some sort of chimera, part male and part female and wholly ridiculous. He got warier around me, not sure whether to praise me for a new outfit or growl at me for getting less than 100 on a math test. There was no way to be both a girl, at least a girl in any normal sense, and a junior version of Dad. Even modest success in one department inevitably meant failure in the other, and failure led regularly to mockery, as in, "Oh, Barb thinks she can cook *too*?" It was damned if you do and damned if you don't, and best to stay out of the way.

If you can't trust your parents and they are intelligent, apparently rational, and au courant, then you can't trust much of anything, and that goes for science as well. Electrons, planets, genes— all these were made suspect, at some deep ontological level, by my parents' endorsement of them. Had I ever seen an electron or even made a careful study of the reasons to think their existence is plausible? Had I gone through the steps to convince myself that a certain point of light in the sky is a planet as opposed to some other bit of space debris? No, of course not. I was completely dependent on scientists for my information about these hypothetical entities, which meant I was assuming that scientists were telling the truth about their observations and inferences and that they were not malign tricksters bent on propagating a massive fiction, nor, for that matter, were they cleverly designed androids in the service of some master trickster. And if I was going to be absolutely rigorous, no assumptions could be permitted at all.

The impetus to set down my first statement of the "facts" was the weekend I spent at a Baptist summer camp, or "resort," to which I had been invited by a Baptist friend. There must be thousands of religious-themed camps like this in the country, aimed at enticing the young with outdoor activities while soothing the elderly with hymns and chicken à la king. This camp featured a dock reaching tentatively out over a light blue lake, or more accurately, pond—never mind that the name of the place promised an ocean beach—and an inordinate amount of prayerful gratitude for the turning of the earth on its axis: O Lord, we thank you for this *day*! I did my best to fit in, bowing my head along with everyone else's and generally zipping my lips so as not to disappoint my friend, who had expressed some shy hopes of saving my soul. Little did she realize how thoroughly her efforts would be undermined by this brief exposure to her coreligionists, as I wrote in my journal:

> As it turned out Ocean Park was no disappointment because I had already prepared for the worst. It was however pleasant swimming etc. but the place is simply run down with superannuated Baptists whose chief subject of conversation is last night's sermon. I am always much more pleased with my family after being away with mental degenerates for a while.

But no sooner did I put down that word "degenerates" than I pulled back in instant remorse, conceding that the campgoers were "clean, honest, and kindly in general." Who was I to judge? And who was really more dogmatic and closed-minded—the Baptists or my parents? In a matter of seconds, my arrogance collapsed into shamefaced humility:

> Whenever I am like this, too critical of the ideas of others and too sure of my own I must remind myself there are only two things that I really know—one: that I exist. I could say I live and am a human being but those things are also matters of definition so I can't be sure. Two: That I know nothing except these two things. One might say that this is being silly and extreme but I think it is best to start out with as few as possible things which you hold to be unquestionably true and start from there.

So there they were—the irrefutable facts from which the rest of the inquiry would have to proceed: *I exist. And I know nothing.*

It would have helped if I'd known something about philosophy beyond its existence and the names of a few notable practitioners, if I'd had any idea that a long line of grown-ups—generally male and wealthy or at least well financed by monarchs—had wrestled with the exact same questions that tormented me. Descartes, for example. I knew of his triumphant foundational statement—"I think, therefore I am"—but I dismissed it as a useless tautology. After all, "I think" means pretty much the same as "I am." You can't think without existing, and you can't express the condition of existing without doing at least a tiny bit of thinking, if only as to which word goes where. What I didn't know at the time was that Descartes had started from the same condition of radical doubt as I had, refusing to accept even sensory data among his "givens," and, equally impressively, refusing to rule out the possibility that the whole thing—the entire universe—is a trick or an optical illusion. Somehow, despite all the peculiarities of my gender, age, class, and family background, I had tapped into the centuries-old mainstream of Western philosophical inquiry, of old men asking over and over, one way or another, *what's really going on here?*

It would have been especially comforting to have all those dead white men by my side when the whole logical enterprise began to come apart, as I suppose it's bound to when you confront the world with only "I" as a given. There's simply no way to get from "I" to "not I" once you've boxed yourself into what I later learned is called Western dualism, with its perpetual divide between mind and matter. Several months into the journal, I began to complain about what I called "circular thoughts," which are just the hall-of-mirrors effect you get when you try to reach the outside world from within the limits of "I." One entry begins without explanation in something like despair:

> If I was confused last time I wrote something I am lost now. I decided to stay calm and not get excited, think objectively etc. That was calming while it lasted, but then it was just another circular thought. I guess the thing to do is to get outside of myself and look in or look around. Of course that is impossible. So I am at an impasse again.

I tried to escape the straitjacket of "I" with a more impersonal formulation: There is Something, and there is Nothing, where Something included both the perceiver (the old "I") and the perceived:

> Any thing which either perceives or is perceived exists and qualifies as Something. Just how much the perceived thing exists is very important to know but I don't see how I ever can. Therefore Nothing has to be just the opposite of Something....Nothing is that which neither perceives nor is perceived.

But then the maddening challenge is to perceive, or comprehend, Nothing—at which point, of course, it gets absorbed into Something, and where are you then?

Even the desire to understand had to be questioned, because desire, when closely examined, makes no sense:

> It seems to me that the principal psychological factor in living things is desire. Reason is purely intellectual (natch) but desire is so basic that it is never explained in any book about psychology I have read. The problem is: is the purpose, essence, of desire *no*

desire (as it certainly seems to be) or is the purpose in the incompleted [unfulfilled?] desire? Is the purpose of life death—or is it in living? Desire seems to be an unsatisfied longing for its own absence, in fact it is.

Page after claustrophobic page of the journal is filled with these paradoxes, with the "real world" as my parents styled it, making an appearance largely as a background annoyance: "If Someone or Something set out to make a universe and I am given an instant in eternity to live in it why is there dirty snow in the gutters, or dishes to do, or homework or clothes or movies or any of this?" Maybe the whole logical enterprise was flawed, and you couldn't really say "this *or* that," "true or false," "one thing or another." In the absence of Hegelian dialectics, which I had not yet encountered, I experimented briefly with a kind of indeterminacy: "Nothing Is Absolutely True or Untrue." But of course that didn't work either, because: "If that is true then it must apply to itself also which means that something is true and its antithesis untrue. Which is right back where I think I started from."

So this great project of *thinking*—where exactly had it gotten me to? The most flattering spin I can put on this phase of paradoxes and metaphysical tangles is that I was smart enough, at age fourteen, to destroy any fledgling hypothesis I came up with. A tentative explanation, theory, or formulation would pop up in my brain only to be attacked by what amounted to a kind of logical immune system, bent on eliminating all that was weak or defective. Which is to say that my mind had become a scene of furious predation, littered with the half-eaten corpses of vast theories and brilliant syntheses. I was a failure at the one unique task I had been given. I existed all right, but I existed only as a condition of constant desiring and yearning, because I *knew* nothing.

God saved Descartes from falling into a similar morass, or, more precisely, Descartes invoked God—in this case, a literal deus ex machina—to save himself. Confronted with the possibility that the universe might make no sense at all, that it might turn out to be a massive deception perpetrated by a demonic deceiver-God, Descartes said, in effect: Whoa, God is perfect, by definition, meaning also perfectly good, so he cannot be a "deceiver." In his benevolence, Descartes's God must have kindly arranged for our perception of things to correspond to their true inner nature, leaving us free to reason our way to the ultimate truth. I couldn't understand the God part of this, but I had some sympathy for what Descartes wanted, and what he wanted was for everything, underneath all the chaos and contradictions, to just be okay.

For a period of four to six months when I was fourteen and fifteen, I too was soothed by religion, though not of the God-ridden variety. I had always been fascinated by religion—meaning the ambient Christianity—as a kind of prefab metaphysics requiring no intellectual effort on the part of the user, and I returned to the subject many times in my journal. Good daughter of atheists that I was, I rejected the part about the universe being administered by some distant parental figure, but I was drawn to the drama of Christianity, with its primal substrate of violence and sacrifice. In practice, however, Christianity was another matter. Whenever I entered its physical precincts, such as the Congregational church I had joined in order to play on its girls' basketball team, I found the same crushingly bland aesthetic that prevailed at school, only with pictures of Jesus instead of flags. "Modern Protestantism," I wrote, "is a social organization, providing basketball, badminton, bowling, dancing and a Sunday fashion show. The most incongruous thing I ever saw in 'our' church was a girl praying. I was startled, really."

Catholicism, with its special effects, its stained glass windows and incense, was a little more intriguing. I understood that it aimed to transport its adherents to some alternative dimension above the dull brick surface of Lowell, but in aiming for the transcendent, it managed, for me at least, to achieve only the weird. I was trying to blend in at one of those sweaty CYO Friday night dances I occasionally went to with a girlfriend, where my goal was neither to dance—because I didn't know how to—nor to be seen not dancing, when it occurred to me that this was a religion whose central ritual was an enactment of cannibalism. I formally renounced Christianity, in writing, on New Year's Eve 1956:

> Now I am sure about religion. Positive. Before I used to think that maybe there was something important in Christianity for me. Once I was impressed by a sign on a car which said "The Answer Is God." Then I realized I had a choice between a life of faith, trusting always in a paternal guardian and submitting to a sort of parental supervision—or being alone. The latter is superficially more difficult, involving the knowledge that when one dies, one is dead, and that it is possible that life is purposeless. My decision, accompanied by much mental fanfare, was easy....

How I came across Hinduism is not recorded. Certainly I had no Hindu friends, nor had the subject ever been mentioned in school, where the boundaries of the known world pretty much coincided with those of the Roman Empire at its height, with the addition of the United States. India, with its swarming beggars and bustling pantheon, its great nonviolent struggle for independence, its caste system and so forth, was not in the syllabus, and the word "curry" had arisen only as a verb. But somehow I acquired a paperback edition of the Upanishads, and within a few months after the above formal rejection of Christianity announced my "conversion" to Hinduism, at least in its most abstract philosophical form, minus all the lurid gods. If all this had happened ten or twenty years later, in the sixties or seventies, it probably would have been Buddhism that I found first. But Hinduism seemed to be my ticket out of Descartes's nightmare of dualism, and fortunately it demanded not the slightest pretense of belief.

Hinduism offered me no epiphanies, only a temporary reassurance. First, it seemed to ratify and even honor my ignorance. "It says in the Upanishads," I noted, "that truly blessed is he who understands the spirit of the words: 'I am not even sure that I know nothing.'" Nor could I expect to know anything, at least not if "knowing" was conceived as an act of conquest in which some sort of mind-creature leaped on its prey. There was no "I" to stalk the "not I" with, only one infinite substance, the Brahman, from whom we were temporarily separated by the thinnest veil of illusion. I was sitting on the little closed-in porch between the kitchen and the back door, reading and half listening to my mother and sister working on dinner, when I laughed out loud— but softly, to myself—in relief. There was no more need to go after the truth like a madman attacking a cliff face with a knife: Everything was already here, complete, and I was coterminous with all of it. All I had to do was give up everything—ambition, desire, curiosity, even, if I were strong enough, dinner.

Naturally I told no one of this sudden "conversion." Maybe I underestimate them, but I'm not sure that my parents' acquaintance with Hinduism extended beyond Kipling, or at best Gandhi. What would I say to them anyway—"Oh, I've gone over to the side of religion, but don't worry, there's no God involved, or at least no single grand monotheistic god"? Since the Upanishads come with no list of instructions—no *pujas*, for example, to perform—I could practice my newfound religion in perfect secrecy, silently repeating "Om," struggling to squelch the desiring self and lift myself beyond the limits of "I."

Part of me desperately wanted to succeed in this project of self-obliteration, in a very direct and physical way. I would be walking back up the hill after school, cherishing the backdrop of bricks and pavement and tiny, ill-tended lawns, which in the absence of woods and fields was my entire exposure to the natural world for the day, when something would come over me—was it a mutant form of the famous "sex drive"?—and make me want to throw myself onto the ground, rub my face into the grass, and be absorbed back into the earth. Wasn't I made of the same stuff myself, although a little heavier on the carbon than the silicon? Didn't I have some kind of "right of return," as the Upanishads seemed to promise? Abolish this flaw in the universe, this membrane separating me from the All, and restore the world to perfect One-ness!

But I never did have to be peeled off somebody's lawn or shaken out of a meditative trance state, and the principal reason was hunger. I might promise myself to skip dinner as an exercise in desirelessness, and the encyclopedia entry on Hinduism had warned me of the travesty of beef. But the prospect of a good hamburger— a little pink in the middle, buns toasted in pan grease—was usually enough to banish all foreign religion. Then there was the other kind of hunger, seemingly issuing from a small shrewlike animal that had made its home inside my head and could never get enough books, ideas, or information to feed on. On the blessed day when *Galaxy* or *Astounding Science Fiction* arrived in the mail, how could I be expected to sit cross-legged on my bed muttering "Om"? And was I really willing to stop asking *why*, which as far as I could see would be indistinguishable from personal death?

There's no point in the journal where I renounce Hinduism;

mentions of it just fade away sometime in 1957. I had glimpsed the vast, glassy-calm, blood-warm sea of Brahman and refused to submerge myself in it. Yes, I knew I was "a part" of this universe, this Something, but also that I was "apart" from it. Beyond dualism and monism there was the inescapable dialectic of "a part" and "apart," which I could not or would not extricate myself from. Besides, I didn't fully trust the Brahman any more than I did Descartes's "perfect God." If consciousness was some sort of defect in an otherwise perfect One-ness, then I wanted that defect to go on a little longer, because without any effort on my part, and apparently independently of my conscious quest, things were beginning to get interesting in a way that nothing I found in the Lowell Public Library had prepared me for.

CHAPTER 3

The Trees Step Out of the Forest

M ost of what I actually wrote in my journal is probably ac-
curate; the problem lies in what I left out, especially in
that first year of entries. Something unspeakable was happening at
irregular intervals beyond my control—unspeakable simply because it came with no words attached. People talk about "leading a
life," as if it were an ox being tugged on a rope through its nose
ring, but in my experience most of what we do is just try to dodge
whatever's coming our way—the blindingly bright, completely unexpected explosions that disrupt even the most orderly plan. No
doubt a responsible narrator would draw a connection between
these shocking intrusions and my desperate attempts to arrive at
"the truth": If you beat your head against a wall for long enough,
either the wall or your head will crack.

The first eight months of journal entries, set in Lowell, contain
just a few indirect references to these uncanny events, allusions
decipherable only by me. I flattered myself that I had made a conscious decision not to write about them out of respect for the
absolutely singularity of what I had experienced. Good schoolgirl
that I was, I reserved the journal for mini-essays on topics like

"chance and determinism," the appeal of religion, "the nature of desire," and whether the passage of time is an illusion. But the truth is I didn't know how to broach the subject and at least understood that any attempt to express the incommunicable risks ending in a sputter of mush.

I can remember perfectly well the first time it happened, about a year before the first journal entry. My mother had determined that we should do something "as a family" on Sunday afternoons, another domestic management strategy that she had gleaned from the women's magazines. No one was exempt from these outings, either by reason of homework or illness, unless they exhibited flamboyant symptoms like fever or vomiting. Mostly, in those days before highways or the perpetual traffic jam of towns, we just squeezed into the car and drove—kids in the back, grown-ups in the front smoking and picking at old sores like the self-answering question of why my father didn't seem to want to spend more time with us. Sometimes there would be a touristic destination or at least a roadside tavern as a turnaround point, where the grown-ups would have a few beers while we kids waited out front. If I had known that drunk driving carried the risk of maiming and death, these Sunday afternoon enterprises might have been more successful at holding my interest. As it was, in the face of stone-cold boredom, there was nothing to do but escape into my personal imaginings.

On this particular Sunday, our destination was a horse show in the town of Hamilton, and I could not tell you even today what was supposed to happen there to warrant the word "show," since neither the animals nor the humans in attendance offered the slightest promise of entertainment. No one in the family had any interest in horses, either as aesthetic objects or as a means of transportation, unless you want to count a near-disastrous attempt on my part to ride the gentle-looking spotted mare that spent her days in a field near our house. I had leaped onto her back from a stone wall—bareback of course because where would I get a saddle from?—a move that prompted the mare's foal to try to kick me off its mother's back, while she in turn launched into a gallop. I managed to leap back off before I was thrown, and scampered away, abashed by my arrogance: What made humans think horses were eager to carry us around with our crotches bouncing against their backs?

The sole attraction of the horse show, to my father anyway, was the chance to sneer at the local gentry, who intruded on our lives, in classic feudal fashion, as landlords. At certain times in the fall they would dress up in jodhpurs and tight-fitted red jackets and "ride to the hounds" through the fields around our house while we watched in amazement from the shelter of a stand of pines. If the horse show was supposed to offer a closer look at the odd equestrian culture of the rich, it failed. There are some extant photos of the occasion still in my sister's possession, showing her, about four years old at the time, toddling through the grass, and my mother sitting at a picnic table, looking off glumly in a direction perpendicular to the camera angle. I had wandered off and was leaning on a fence, staring at the woods in the pale late summer sunlight, feeling nothing but impatience for the passage of time.

And then it happened. Something peeled off the visible world, taking with it all meaning, inference, association, labels, and words. I was looking at a tree, and if anyone had asked, that's what I would have said I was doing, but the word "tree" was gone, along with all the notions of tree-ness that had accumulated in the last dozen or so years since I had acquired language. Was it a place that was suddenly revealed to me? Or was it a substance—the indivisible, elemental material out of which the entire known and agreed-upon world arises as a fantastic elaboration? I don't know, because this substance, this residue, was stolidly, imperturbably mute. The interesting thing, some might say alarming, was that when you take away all human attributions—the words, the names of species, the wisps of remembered tree-related poetry, the fables of photosynthesis and capillary action—that when you take all this away, *there is still something left*.

I snapped out of it soon enough. The faces were reapplied to the heads of my family members; the trees crept back into the woods; we reassembled for the drive home. After what I remember as a muted dinner, probably because I just wasn't listening, I went up to the bedroom I shared with my sister to assess and regroup. Some fundamental sense of entitlement had been challenged, that much was clear, because surely I deserved—everyone in fact deserved—something better than a world without meaning, and I wasn't even so sure about a world containing occasional meaning-free patches to stumble on.

That was the deal, wasn't it? We live out our little lives, then we die, but the payoff was supposed to be some glorious meaning, for anyone clever enough to find it, that would light up the sky, perhaps at the moment of death, like the aurora borealis, and redeem all the trivia and suffering. That's what "meaning" is—a special additive like salt or garlic that could make the most fetid piece of meat seem palatable, even delicious. On my bedside table lay, as usual, *The Pocket Book of Verse*, with Longfellow reminding me, in a poem I could still recite at the time without irony, that "life is real, life is earnest." More to my taste was "Ozymandias," in which Shelley took death and futility head-on and still managed to emerge with human dignity intact. And here was Whitman, page after page of him, tremulous with desire in the lilac-scented night. They were just doing their job, these poets, which is really the job of all of us—to keep applying coat upon coat of human passion and grandiosity to the world around us, trying to cover up whatever it is that lies underneath.

So I decided that evening that whatever I had experienced at the horse show had to be an aberration, like the retinal floaters that sometimes intruded on my vision after being in the car too long on a hot bright day. I hadn't had enough sleep the night before, no more than three or four hours, that was the problem. A chronic insomniac since grade school, I often read at night until my eyes were too tired to read anymore and then lay there in terror of being caught still awake by the dawn. Sleep deprivation does odd things to the mind, and this must be one of them. It was curious, but so were a lot of other things.

Except that it kept happening, not only when I was overtired, and it gained legitimacy through repetition. I might be in school, concentrating on Latin conjugations or logarithmic tables, and suddenly notice my fingers holding the pencil and realize I was looking at a combination of yellow and pink, of straight and curved, that had never been seen before and never would be seen again by anyone in the universe, not in this precise configuration anyway, and with that realization, all that was familiar would drain out of the world around me. Or I might look up from a book to find a patch of sunlight pulsing on the floor and feel it leap up to challenge the solidity of the entire scene. Sometimes, I wrote:

> I am quite sure that this is not real, so sure that I am completely
> absorbed and come back with difficulty. Then it seems to be unreal
> simply because it is so improbable. At times like that I am not even
> real to myself. I don't know where I am. My own thoughts are like
> a distant throbbing whisper. It is as if I am only consciousness and

not an individual, both a part of and apart from my environment. Strange. Everything looks strange as if I'd never seen it before.

It could happen when I was alone or it could happen with other people, including family and friends. I could be in the midst of a conversation with a friend, for example, when "without warning my sense of reality changed, and her image and voice and presence along with everything else seemed to slip like water off a sheet of glass."

I struggled to identify precipitating factors, if not physiological, then atmospheric. One thing became clear within a couple of months: Nothing untoward was going to happen at night or if it was raining or the sky was overcast, which meant that for about nine months of the year I was insulated or, as I was also coming to see it, locked out. Why sunlight was so important I still don't know. I have read that some odd mental states can be triggered by light, although usually by flashing or strobe lights. In my case, no flashes are required. When the sun, especially the afternoon sun, slants at a certain angle or gets refracted through venetian blinds or bounced off walls of bricks—well, there's not much that I can do but wait quietly and see what's going to be revealed.

If there was any other pattern to these occurrences it was that they tended to happen at a point of liminality, usually the borderline between absorption in one thing, like Latin verbs, and another, like a pencil. I imagine that everyone has experienced the momentary disorientation that comes from being roused from concentration on a book or a complicated line of thought. Maybe I just had more trouble navigating these transitions than other people, and got stuck in the in-between place, where I would loiter for a moment and look around. Or maybe other people had the same experience exactly and just flicked it away like a fly, because what's the point of seeing something you can't say anything about or even trying to recall something that can't be recalled, that will only come back when it decides to recur?

I had no rubric under which to store these things; even the phrase "altered states of consciousness" would not be invented for another decade, and "mental illness" never entered my mind until a few years later. If I had any literary reference point in that first year, it was Prince Myshkin in *The Idiot*, whose epileptic fits were preceded by flashes of blinding lucidity, which were intriguing enough but hardly analogous to my experience, seeming to involve, as they did, so many obscure insights into Christianity and Russian nationalism. So I came up with my own explanation, patched together from the fragments of psychology I had picked up at the library, which suggested that the most routine perception requires an impressive creative effort. Photons don't just stamp a little image on the visual cortex, captioned with a word like "tree." You have to do some work—comparing one pattern of neuronal firing to another, sifting through the stored images that are your memories until you have a match, and so forth:

It occurred to me in so many words that what constitutes reality are the sensa perceived by our eyes, ears, etc. which are actually made up in the mind or should I say brain? So they are certainly not to be relied upon to any extent. At the time I thought this was a really radical thought and now I find it in books. So it was pretty important especially since I thought it independently. Bertrand Russell says that introspection is just as unreliable so now I don't know where I am.

So from a scientific perspective, what happened to me was that every now and then I simply stopped doing the work of perception and refused to transform the hail of incoming photons into named and familiar objects. There was plenty of input still pouring in in the form of sounds and colors and lights, but it wasn't getting sorted and categorized. This was my theory anyway—that I was just falling down on my job as a conscious human being, sort of like going on strike. Instead of attacking, say, trees with all the word power at my disposal, or dismissing them as too routine to merit attention and moving on to the next thing, I had let them run wild and speak for themselves. I, the point of consciousness tasked with organizing sensory data into a coherent reality, had temporarily ceased to exist. And whatever I saw, or thought I saw, during these episodes was of no more significance than an optical illusion.

But I wasn't ready to abandon the idea that I had gained a privileged glimpse into some alternative realm or dimension. It wasn't a "place" of course—a Narnia or Land of Oz—but science fiction and bits of pop science gave the metaphor a degree of plausibility. In sci-fi there were always multiple worlds to travel between by rocket ship or subtler technologies, and science held forth alternative dimensions, folded up and hidden within our own world. So one way to look at what was going on was to imagine another universe, intimately superimposed on our own, normally invisible, but every so often, where the dividing membrane had worn thin, shining through into our own. I was lucky enough to have some intermittent access to this place, though not at my own volition. Just now and then, maybe every few weeks and then only for minutes at a time, a breach appeared in the partition and I walked on through, because I have always taken that as a general rule of life: If a door opens, walk on through and at least take a look around.

Rationality favored the perceptual breakdown theory, but it wasn't mysticism that pulled me in the other direction. I was adamantly disinclined to anything that smacked of mysticism, unless you want to count my abstract and colorless version of Hinduism. But I was also an empiricist, and empiricism is one of the great pillars of science. You can and should use logic and reason all you want. But it would be a great mistake to ignore the stray bit of data that doesn't fit into your preconceived theories, that may even confound everything you thought you were sure of. I had seen what I had seen—whatever it is that lies under the named world—and I was not going to deny its existence.

There is a word for this, the episodes I was experiencing, though it was not available to me at the time: "dissociation," described in the psychiatric literature as "feeling unreal," either that one is unreal or that the world around one is unreal, if those two conditions can even be distinguished. If the episodes of dissociation happen often enough, they achieve the official status of a disease or at least a "disorder"—"dissociative disorder," a.k.a. "depersonalization" or "derealization disorder," which may be accompanied by a variety of other symptoms, including emotional numbness, depression, or amnesia, none of which afflicted me. You can find all this in the latest *Diagnostic and Statistical Manual of Mental Disorders*, where dissociative disorder is described as a general cognitive breakdown, "a disruption in consciousness, memory, identity, or perception. In other words, one of these areas is not working correctly." More ominously, the current online *Encyclopedia of Human Illnesses and Behavioral Health* offers the following explanation of schizophrenia, a disorder that, it is said, frequently features dissociation:

Information in the form of electrical signals flows down nerve cells in the brain, triggering the release of neurotransmitters. These chemical messengers transmit information from one nerve cell to another. In healthy people, neurotransmitter traffic usually flows smoothly....In people with schizophrenia, however, neurotransmitter traffic runs into major roadblocks, unscheduled stops, and unmapped detours to frightening and unreal places. These traffic disruptions result in periods of psychosis, during which people with schizophrenia lose touch with healthy reality and seem to get trapped in alternate realities. With anti-psychotic medication, people with schizophrenia often find their way back to the healthy realities of everyday life.

In other words, "incorrect" perceptions may reveal "frightening," "unreal," or unhealthy "alternate" realities, but these can generally be banished with drugs.

I suspected even at the time that my episodes of dissociation in some way constituted a punishable offense. Prince Myshkin ended up back in the sanitarium, didn't he?—and there was no shortage of mental hospitals in Massachusetts in the 1950s, menacing dark brick buildings to enclose the people who refused to do what was expected of them or who said things that didn't make sense. This was still a few years before my mother and her sister Jean underwent their stints—voluntary and otherwise—in mental wards, for what we would today call depression and was endemic at the time to women who were full-time homemakers. But I did remember a particularly vacant-looking neighbor in Pittsburgh who, as my mother explained, had been subjected to shock treatment because she hadn't been making dinner or cleaning the house—tasks that presumably became much more manageable once the neuronal circuitry had been shocked back into submission.

Nothing like that could happen to me, because I did everything that was expected of me and, outside of the housework department, did it fairly well: I set my hair nightly in the skull-denting metal curlers my mother provided me with. I was up every morning with homework completed, appropriately dressed and ready for school. I babysat three or four times a week and spent most of my earnings on records—classical, but intensely romantic, with an occasional venture into jazz—and subscriptions to sci-fi periodicals. But if I never imagined myself qualifying for incarceration, I did worry about committing what amounts to treason where my family was concerned. Whatever was revealed in my dissociative episodes seemed to mock both my mother's commitment to "realism" and my father's fascination with the solidity of minerals. Human beings are connected not only by love and loyalty—or, more generally, by neurotic symbiosis and material dependency—but by our joint agreement about the "real." It's what we share—the rock there by my foot, that little white cloud in the sky—amounting in sum to the grand project of "empirical reality," which I was expected to contribute to as a scientist when I grew up. Step outside the borders of what is "real" and collectively agreed upon and you might as well fall right off the planet into a personal orbit of your own.

Hinduism cannot be blamed for luring me into the trackless wilds. Chronologically, my "conversion" came months after the experience of dissociation was well established, and what I wanted most from Hinduism was simply *access*, a way to get to the "other place" when I wanted, not just when it chose to make itself available, which was not often enough in the long, dark winters of Lowell. I had hoped that the discipline of meditation would achieve this, but reciting "Om" seemed to lead in a different direction, at least as far as I could tell from the Upanishads, since I never could stick to it long enough to find out for myself—toward the numbness of universal perfection, or something closely resembling boredom.

There was one point when I badly wanted to talk about my perceptual excursions. In the fall of 1956, only a few weeks after I had begun to keep the journal, I had an argument with my friend Bernice during one of our Latin tutoring sessions. Bernice was not automatically seen by the school as college material, due to the fact that she lacked the hereditary credentials that I was granted by virtue of my father's white-collar status. Her parents ran a tiny coffee shop in downtown Lowell, above which the family made their home and where she and I often copped a free doughnut before school. She was good enough company for at least about an hour a day, but we were friends mainly by default, since Lowell high school culture was segregated into the Irish, the "French," and a tiny handful of Jews, none of whom made me welcome at their lunch tables. This left me with the Greeks, like Bernice, who in their own way were outsiders too, and when she determined to win a place in the "academic track" by mastering Latin—the language of her nation's ancient Roman conquerors, I couldn't help noticing—I had offered to help.

How exactly the subject of God came up this time I don't know, since we had already gone over this ground before and I had thought we could leave it at that. She would tell me it was unnatural not to believe and I would tell her that she was making an unnatural demand. Belief takes effort. Why should I exert the effort required to believe that she, Bernice, was at all times accompanied by an invisible person or personage? A person whose sole attribute was perfection—all goodness, all love, and all reason? Was I supposed to lie and say, "Oh yes, I know who you're talking about—I can see him there, right over your shoulder, or at least the gleam of an impossible radiance"?

Or she would accuse me of immorality, because how could anyone be moral without God to guide and reward them? This I could handle, since I had already determined, after great deliberation, that the things Christians counted as "sins" were not things I would want to do anyway, and that the only principle to go by was kindness—"doing unto others," etcetera. The Ten Commandments, for example, were no more challenging than the Girl Scout oath, and why should anyone be tempted to put one false god ahead of another?

Our dispute this time arose over the declension of the Latin word *deus*, for god, which I emphasized—completely unnecessarily and pedantically, I admit—*could* be declined. That is, it had a plural as well as a feminine form, so at least to the Romans, "god" was not some singular point of light, but a whole category of beings, none of whom qualified as moral exemplars: Jupiter and his rages, Juno and her petty jealousies, Venus and her vanity. "So?" Bernice retorted unwisely. "The Romans were pagans." This was of course my opening to point out that the Romans inherited their silly pantheon directly from the ancient Greeks, who were the very inventors of civilization as far as Bernice was concerned. I was not asserting any kind of ethnic superiority here—how could I, knowing that my own ancestors had been painting themselves blue and worshipping oak trees while hers were coming up with the Pythagorean theorem? But I may have needled her a bit here— again, out of sheer intellectual wickedness—for trading in her colorful ancient polytheistic tradition for this ghostly abstraction of a God she wanted me to "believe" in.

She struck back with surprising vehemence, her dark brown eyes going hard with reproof: It wasn't just that atheists were immoral; they were "shallow" and trapped in the commonplace, while she and her fellow believers had access to some transcendent dimension. I don't know what the exact words were here, but the point was that I was missing something, left out, just grubbing around among the superficial surfaces of things. Banality—that

was the problem with atheists—and as she said this I could feel banality weighing down on me like some huge sodden pig that had
draped itself over the roof of our house, over all roofs actually, and
most of the sky in between.

I reached for the only weapon that came to hand—the flabby,
soft-minded notion of the "spiritual," which I at least had the good
taste to acknowledge in my journal as a "poor word, but you know
what I mean." What I was groping for was a concept that would
embrace both her religion and my adventures in perception—both
the incense-driven mystery of the Orthodox rite and the stark
beauty of the place that lay beyond words. There are spiritual insights, I told Bernice, that have nothing to do with religion.

Oh yeah, she wanted to know, what are they? Because for her,
the "spiritual" was not just some delicate mist arising from the
church steeples. It had a face and a name and could be evoked
through precise ritual procedures. If I had these supposed "spiritual insights," could I recount or explain them?

No, of course I couldn't—later writing that "I could not would
not shall not tell her." And what *would* I have told her, if I'd had
the courage or the verbal skills to do anything but stonewall? That
the things we each held to be true—her religion as well as my athe-
istic, Latin-loving rationalism—were both capitulations to what
might be, for all we knew, some monstrous hoax? That they were
inventions of the human imagination with no obvious grounding
in what I was increasingly, and despite my tenacious rationalism,
coming to see as the "real"?

So I ceded the fight to Bernice, who went home in triumph,
leaving me, still steaming, to ask my mother, who was busy in the
kitchen making dinner: Could something be true but not explainable? Of course not, she said. If you can't explain something it isn't
true and has no basis in fact, which I took to mean that in her view

all human experience maps perfectly to *Webster's Dictionary*. What isn't in it isn't there. Everything that humans can experience has already been named, alphabetized, and stored in a single volume, supplemented of course by the *Encyclopedia Americana*. I drew my own conclusion, which was that there is an entire category of experience that is not suited to intraspecies communication, so you are advised to keep it to yourself.

I attempted to sort things out that night in my journal, in one long, knotted paragraph on the human need to feel superior, written so impersonally that it's possible to read it as either arrogance or apology. "Everyone," I observed, "thinks he or she is unique and likes to think that he possesses great powers of perception and is of uncommonly profound nature." For the religious, God was the ticket:

> Man believes himself to be the special creation of his most alarming invention and servant, God. God is an extension of human personality brought into the world and enslaved as man's glorifier. God is the final superiority that humans can conceive for their selfish delight.

But where did I get *my* edge from, my sense of being special, or, as we would later say (the word had yet to be invented), my "self-esteem"? Certainly not from being more beautiful, more athletic, or smarter than other people, although I acknowledged I was a little smarter than many. No, it was from the "very important things" I knew, or inferred, from my unique access to the world as it "really" was—things that even my genius father did not seem to know, and I was not going to share them with "any old clod" like Bernice.

This is embarrassing, but, objectively, also interesting. If dissociation/depersonalization is a symptom of a "disorder," then you might expect the experience to cause some pain. Go to the "Depersonalization Community" at dpselfhelp.com, and that's what you'll find: one report after another of agonizing detachment, failed treatments, or long, slow slogs back to a shaky "normality." A woman complains, for example, of "weird abstract thoughts like what is that fan/carpet/doll/plane made of and why the f@#k is it here?" and then goes on to ask, "Why do I have to be sick/why doesn't anyone I know understand/how am I supposed to deal with this/do I go to a doctor for a health check-up or accept it as a mental disorder?" And much more like that, leaving me to conclude that self-identified victims of "DPD" have radically different reactions to dissociation than I did. Was I exempted from the menace of pathology simply by my ignorance about mental illness? I don't know, but what they seek to be cured of—the "weird abstract thoughts" and so forth—I took as a special privilege. And even today, as an apparently sane and responsible grown-up, it seems to me that a person who questions the reality of objects and can ask why "the f@#k" they're here is a philosopher, not a mental patient.

True, as a psychiatrist might have noted, my social connections were a little thin on the ground at the time when I started to dissociate. Bernice was not the only friend or potential friend repelled by my atheism; there may have been, in heavily Catholic Lowell, a conscious boycott for all I know. At the same time, my siblings disappeared, both from my journal and my sight, seduced by the arrival of television, which had the effect of making them seem dumber and me, no doubt, seem more priggish and aloof to them. I had had only one crush on a boy, and that had ended badly with him joining the other boys on the school bus in taunting me for my pimples and general oddness. In fact it was around this time that I started using "other people" as an analytic category, distinct from me and distinct from "things." What I hadn't been able to tell Bernice during our conversation about God was that it was hard enough for me to believe in *her*—that is, to believe that behind her face and voice and gestures there was a conscious being just like myself, or perhaps unlike me and alien in ways I could not imagine. Believing in her, or even my family members for that matter, as independent minds took all the effort I could muster. Cause and effect are not easy to separate here: Did I "dissociate" because I was estranged or did the dissociative episodes drive a wedge between me and all my kind? Logic favored the latter explanation. If I questioned the reality of physical objects, how could I so readily attribute mind and consciousness and feeling to other people, who were, in the most general sense, physical objects too, although of a cleverly animated sort?

If I needed anything from the grown-up world, it was not some concerned professional to interrogate my feelings and direct my metaphysics onto a presumably healthier and more productive track. I needed better teachers or perhaps a kindly librarian to point out that books are meant to be consumed in a certain order and not all at once. There are invisible lines connecting them: First you learn some physics, *then* you can daydream about quantum physics or antimatter. First Kant, *then* Hegel and Nietzsche. On the whole, despite family tensions, social isolation, the ongoing horror of puberty, and intermittent philosophical despair, I was not unhappy, or if I was, I did not see fit to write about it. There was too much going on for that, too much to find out and absorb, and emotions were not my natural beat. I was an answer-seeking machine, in love with what I called "the truth," whether it came in the form of little truth particles stuck to the pages of books or vast patterns screaming out from the obvious and mundane. At the same time, I was overwhelmed by the aesthetic runoff from adolescence—the shameless beauty of the world, regenerated each day as if by magic, without any help from me. Lowell, all coppery in the winter sunrise, looked "like a Sumerian city on the banks of the Tigris or Euphrates," while the junior girls' calisthenics class was a "dance of priestesses of the sun." "These things fascinate me," I wrote when I was sixteen:

> bees, straight lines, the ocean, the idea that every word is an ex-ample of onomatopoeia (sp?), the music of Tchaikovsky, Liszt, Borodin, Ravel, Debussy, ancient Egypt, other planets, the idea that the stars as I see them are not only trillions of miles away but are millennia ago and may no longer be there, Greenland, people and everything else. I like the line "alone, alone, all, all alone, alone on a wide wide sea."

If this was mental illness, or even just a particularly clinical case of adolescence, I was bearing up pretty well.

CHAPTER 4

A Land without Details

When my father revealed that we would be moving to California in early 1958, where he would have a new job with better pay, my overall feeling was: It's time. "Lowell," I wrote in anticipation of the move, "is the kind of city I like to go through on a train and think how lucky I am not to live there." We'd been there for a year and a half, a longer stopover than usual, and a thin crust of familiarity had already settled on all the churches and buildings and houses. When a place gets all echoey like this, I felt, when everywhere you look you see residues of what's already happened, the only thing to do is move on. The specific content of the memories does not have to be tragic; it's just that no matter how you evoke it, the past is inherently always about death: what was and no longer is. My family had found a surefire way to escape the sickening accretion of memory, which was to pack up and move.

I understood too that the concept of home was badly in need of updating before it expired altogether when I reached eighteen, which was, as my mother had always made clear, when I would "age out" like a foster child and be released to the streets or, should I qualify, to college. This did not seem so harsh to me at the time, since I understood the family, my family at least, to be a temporary and unstable unit like one of those clumsily named elements down at the bottom of the periodic table, Berkelium or Rutherfordium, for example. In the new managerial gypsy class we had entered, the point was not to set down roots—or, in chemical terms, bond with other families or groups—but to follow the breadwinner as unseen forces drove him from one office, one company, one brand to another. And then, when we were no longer needed to provide him with the cover of suburban respectability, the family would undergo fission and we would head off in our separate directions.

By this time it was obvious that my father had given up science—which was the only white-collar occupation he deemed worthy of a person's best efforts—for money. Given that he was over six feet tall, looked like Dean Martin, and could outdrink any competitor, maybe it had been inevitable that he would eventually be drafted from the laboratory into management and what was ultimately, at the time of his retirement in the 1980s, a salary in the upper five figures. Or maybe he fought for his various promotions—hiding the tattoo under neatly pressed white shirts and suit jackets, upgrading from boilermakers to martinis, developing a consistently below-par golf game and an enthusiasm for flying around the country to meetings. The fiction was that he did it all for us. Maudlin with drink one Sunday afternoon, he told me that, left to himself, he would happily have toiled away in the lab, but that he had a family to support, which meant submission to the endless, trivial, and demeaning demands of the company. It would have been easier on me if he had just waved toward the corporate hierarchy he had so much contempt for and said: See this pile of steaming shit? Well, I'm going to climb my way to the top of it.

But I was not too sure about his choice of California. I knew the stereotype, thanks to *Life* magazine, of happy, tanned people driving around in sports cars from one beach party to another. What if all this sunshine worked its magic on me and I turned into a *teenager*? Chronologically, I fit the description, but I knew the demographic group only as the "juvenile delinquents" of media paranoia or the dwarf grown-ups practicing mating rituals on *American Bandstand*. Adolescence I could handle and in fact might as well have been running through a checklist of approved adolescent activities. Read Dostoevsky: Check. Camus: Check. Escape into fugue states where the agreed-upon and shared reality of world evaporates: Check.…In Lowell, I could move seamlessly from school to family dinner to an evening immersion in *The Underground Man* without experiencing the slightest hiccup of dissonance. But who could read Dostoevsky in a subtropical environment or Conrad in a place where the major seafaring activity seemed to be surfing? I arrived in Los Angeles with my shoulders hunched against the threat of corruption.

It was different all right, but not always in the ways I expected. This was my first exposure to the "modern," by which I don't mean anything fancy and academic; that's just the word my parents used to describe what they saw as the upgrade in our new environment. Lowell had been ancient and gnarly; in Los Angeles, or at least on the white west side of the city where we took up residence, everything was clean and smooth. Gone were the curlicues and doodads that adorned Lowell's nineteenth-century building façades, replaced by plain, flat, pastel-colored walls that seemed to have no function at all except to reflect back the sun. I found this modernity immensely freeing, at first anyway: an invitation to fill in the blanks for myself.

Gone too were the churches; at least they were not prominent in the suburban scenery of West L.A. at the time. If I wanted to reflect on the glories and shortcomings of organized religion, there were no cathedrals to sit in quietly for purposes of observation, but I could walk just twenty minutes from our house down Sunset Boulevard to something called the "Church of All Religions," which was my first clue as to the essential strangeness of L.A., apart from the climate. Here the religions were all conveniently on display together, each represented by its own shrine or plaque, and organized around a little freshwater lake, the only one in Los Angeles. Well, not all religions. Christianity and Hinduism were the most prominently represented, and each of them only in its softest, most loving form, suggesting that the essence of religion is one long swoon into the infinite All. Nothing like this "church" could have occurred in New England, of course, where the denominations bristled with mutual hostility and the realm of the sacred never bore any resemblance to an amusement park. The Church of All Religions had once been a movie set—perhaps for the filming of a version of *Don Quixote*, since the most prominent feature of the site was a windmill—and had later been taken over by a successful ecumenically minded swami. The most memorable aspect of Hinduism here was the plaque revealing that for weeks after his death the swami's corpse had remained sweet-smelling and his nails had continued to grow.

Even the city's sprawl delighted me, testifying as it did to an excess of space. Stores didn't have to be crammed into the first floor of multistory buildings housing stacks of offices higher up. In fact, there were hardly any offices or office buildings visible at all, suggesting that whatever was going on here—the shiny diners, supermarkets, and shopping centers—had sprung up spontaneously and without any kind of administrative oversight. High school wasn't a single grim box of a building, it was a "campus" of scattered bungalows, one for each teacher or class, and you could walk right on out to the parking lot and, if you had learned how to smoke, have a cigarette, with no one paying any attention. In my last few weeks in Lowell, a girl had been dragged into the basement of the high school and raped—a crime so awful it could only be whispered and then only by a determined "realist" like my mother. Nothing like that could happen at my new high school, where there was no basement or dark interstitial spaces to get trapped in.

I was right to be on guard, though. We arrived in March, the middle of a semester, leaving me scrambling to catch up in trigonometry, which as a result I never fully understood. What kind of person looks at, say, a piece of rhubarb pie and comes up with the notion of a cosine? What is the deep mysterious link between triangles and circles, sharp points and gentle curves? Even more threatening was a required course brazenly entitled "Life Adjustment," since I knew that just by looking at me anyone could tell I fell short of "adjustment." Most of my clothes were homemade by my mother, like the Black Watch plaid dress with the white appliqué collar and cuffs that I had been so proud of in Lowell, but that here, where the cool girls wore close-fitting sweaters and tight tubular skirts, looked like some kind of folk costume. On about my third session in this course we were given a "personality test" to fill out, featuring multiple-choice questions about our eagerness to spend time with friends (of which I had none at the moment), eventual interest in marriage, and general satisfaction with the status quo. I filled it out quickly and guilelessly, prepared to learn something about that mysterious doppelgänger, my "personality." But no, as soon as we had finished the tests, the teacher instructed us to exchange papers with the person sitting across the aisle from us, so that the tests could be *corrected*.

I stuck up my hand to raise the obvious, even platitudinous question: How could there be "right" answers if, as had just been explained, each person has a unique personality? All the time thinking: What is this, *communism*? Because as I understood it, that's what communism, our great national enemy, meant—the forcible destruction of the individual by the power of the state— and here it was going on right out in the open. I got some kind of patronizing answer about my being new to the class and how everything would be clear soon enough. So I stood up without saying another word, picked up my books, and walked out of the bungalow, taking my potentially incriminating test with me. The amazing thing, compared to what might have happened in Lowell, is that I *could* just walk out, without anyone trying to stop me.

By the end of the day, this seemed less like a moment of glorious resistance than a narrow escape. I understood that my test answers were seriously wrong, off the scale, possibly insane, and that I would be exposed as a deviant with no place in this sunny, superficially friendly new world. When I got home I went to my room and broke into tears. It's too late now to perform a chemical assay and determine how much these were the hot tears of a fresh hurt and how much the familiar balm of childish self-pity, but there was definitely hurt involved. I had come to believe, especially as the acne subsided in the last year or so, that it was up to me to decide how much to be involved with the growing category of "other people," with Joseph Conrad weighing in heavily on the side of involvement. He had convinced me, in story after story, that tragedy awaits the person who fails to reach out in love, to make a commitment to other people or even just a connection. There it was in *Victory*: "Woe to the man whose heart has not learned while young to love, to hope—to put its trust in life," to take the plunge, in other words, that Conrad's hero takes far too late. In my journal, I had chided myself more than once for my aloofness, even finding it "deplorable," and promised to correct it someday when the opportunity arose to develop "emotional involvements."

But now the personality test raised the possibility that the choice might not be mine to make. Maybe I had been in the wilderness for too long and developed some rude odor that no one expects to find indoors. What with all that reading, thinking, and staying up late to make notes, I had let myself go, failed to keep up my credentials as a human being, and turned into the kind of freak who had to be ejected from human society lest the general consensus be undone. I did not belong here, as sooner or later the school officials and everyone else would realize.

I dried my eyes, went back downstairs, and cautiously announced to my mother that California was not working out for me; it was obvious that I didn't fit in. What was I expecting— pity? California wasn't working for her either. My father was rarely around and she had left all her civic attachments in Lowell, where by the end of our stay she had risen to the presidency of the citywide PTA. So she just smacked the iron down hard on the handkerchief she was ironing for the sole purpose of enabling it to stick neatly out from my father's breast pocket and told me that I had always thought I was "special" and that was what was wrong with me, because I wasn't special at all. I was just like everyone else and I might as well get used to it.

Nevertheless I managed, with no help from my parents, to transfer out of Life Adjustment. The next day I went to the administration office, housed in a bungalow of its own, where I announced to some adult at a desk that I could not take this course, that it went against my most fundamental principles. She kindly allowed me to switch to typing, which I had failed to learn when I went from "typing practice" to longhand journal-keeping. Possibly she took me for some kind of hard-line Christian who found

Life Adjustment offensively secular by virtue of its inattention to the afterlife.

After that I stopped worrying about being a deviant and began to think of myself in a new way, as a rebel, and no one, however psychiatrically or politically conservative, should hold this against me, because at least it was a halting step toward social connectedness, an acknowledgment that there *were* other people and that I existed in some kind of relationship to them. I fit into the human enterprise after all, even if my role was to overthrow it from within. I laid this out a few months after our arrival in Los Angeles, in an entry I submitted to a newspaper essay contest on the theme of "the role of youth in our society" or a similar abstraction that could only have been crafted in an era when newspaper editors suffered from an excess of job security. Unfortunately no copy of my essay survives, but the general idea was that "society" tends toward stagnation and conformity unless continually challenged by the young. That was it: no complaints about racial injustice or nuclear war, neither of which loomed large in my metaphysical scheme of things, just a general exhortation to stand up, question everything, take nothing for granted. I comforted myself when I lost with the fact that I would not have accepted the prize anyway, which was a date with the young actor who had starred in a movie called *The Restless Years*.

What I was rebelling against? Well, of course the great collectivist project of high school, which was to transform us all into interchangeable units capable of occupying the interchangeable houses that made up Southern California suburbia. I learned to smoke, which I didn't have to go outside of the family to master, since my beloved aunt Jean, on a rare visit, introduced me to her menthol-flavored Newports, from which I graduated to stealing my parents' Camels. Smoking came in handy for waiting out high school's most fascist institution—football "pep rallies" at which attendance was mandatory. Kathy, one of my first California friends, and I would hide in adjacent stalls in a girls' restroom and pass a cigarette back and forth while the sound of brainwashed chanting poured in through the window. We thought that if we stood on the toilet seats no one would see us by looking under the doors. It did not occur to us, at that point in the history of American public health, that cigarette smoke had a detectable odor.

Or you could say that I was rebelling against banality, but only if you understood by banality the near-universal refusal to recognize "the situation," including the impending deaths of all of us. It made me almost frantic that everyone could go on doing what they were doing without ever acknowledging what was going on— the steady turning of the earth and passage of days, leading, as far as anyone could tell, to the absolute darkness of Nothing. That first summer in Los Angeles, while I was taking physics in summer school and polishing up my French by reading Gide's *La porte étroite*, I wrote:

> Very often in a classroom or a conversation I feel like yelling, "What difference does it make?" Because 94% of my life is occupied with utter trivia. Much of my rebelliousness starts with indifference to what is urgently important to others. Being constantly subjected to it at school, at work [I had a phone-answering job for a TV repair service], I feel like screaming and throwing things.

In school I made a few friends that first semester, mostly bright, studious, college-bound kids like myself to eat lunch with and occasionally see after school. It was easy to make friends here, where people did not sort themselves by religion, and where no one was impressed, one way or another, by my atheism, or intent on converting me. A school of this size even offered a small selection of fellow misfits like Kathy, who was rich and self-assured enough to giggle at the monstrous expectation that we fit into some Hollywood teenage norm. I lived not far from David—poor, chronically morose David—who would have been my boyfriend if such a concept had ever arisen between us. We got together at his house after school, where there was an actual bar in the living room, and if no one was around we would sit cross-legged on the floor and sample his parents' liquor while we talked about something like furniture: What did it really add to anything? Why did people submit to such an obvious obstruction and burden? There was my first-ever "political" friend, Dina, a Zionist who had spent a year in a kibbutz and glowed with an incomprehensible zeal for agrarian socialism.

Mostly there was Marina, who daringly wore peasant skirts and hoop earrings to school, and introduced me to the nascent concept of bohemia. I spent more time with her than any other friend, often at her house, which featured an enviably jolly mother and bright, crude, folkish weavings on the walls. Sometimes we studied chemistry together, or at least laughed about it, gleefully naming the day of a major upcoming test—it fell on Friday, April 26— Black Faraday, we called it, in honor of the nineteenth-century chemist Michael Faraday. It was Marina who located the first coffeehouse we ventured out to in Venice, ostensibly in search of folk music. Sometimes someone would take out a guitar and make sounds that I would strain to appreciate while Marina nodded along rapturously. What impressed me most about these places was that nothing was for sale. Hot water and instant coffee were available on a table near the entrance, and you could leave some change in a jar if you felt like it. Contrast that to the diner where I now waitressed on weekends and evenings, where in principle every sugar cube had to be accounted for.

My parents didn't know about our forays into L.A.'s emerging "beat" scene (which didn't call itself that—or anything), and this was a good thing since the newspaper seemed to think it was a hotbed of "narcotics" and sexual "deviancy." Actually there was more so-called deviancy at the diner I worked in, where the ultra-butch middle-aged fry cook had begun giving me long inquiring looks, especially around closing time. I admired her proficiency as a cook, but if she had another life to go home to, a smaller and possibly more squalid kitchen of her own, I did not want to know about it.

Drugs, yes, there were no doubt some drugs in the coffeehouse culture. Marina and I became friendly with Frank, a guitar player who was our age and went on to become a rock star in the sixties— as I realized years later only when I saw one of his album covers. I was driving my mother's car when Marina, in the passenger seat, opened the paper bag on her lap to show me that it was filled with a flaky brown substance she identified as Frank's marijuana, which for some reason he'd asked Marina to hold on to for him. I insisted, over her baffled objections, that we pull over and dump it down a storm drain—before the police caught us, or before we were tempted to try it and descend immediately into delinquency and ruin.

The real danger of the nascent counterculture was nothing more than the spectacle of grown-ups openly shirking their grown-up responsibilities, sitting around for hours without any visible connection to jobs or offices or factories or families. This was immensely reassuring to me, like finding a pocket of people who'd survived a deadly disease I had just been diagnosed with: Becoming an adult at, say, age eighteen didn't have to mean giving up everything you cared about and getting press-ganged into a life of domestic service. You could sit in a coffeehouse all day and late into the night if you wanted to, smoking, chatting, drinking bitter coffee, and maybe playing a game of chess. Though there was always the question of what sustained these people in a material sense—whether they had homes and self-renewing bank accounts or slept on the beach. There was no way to judge by the way anyone looked.

I admired Marina, more so than any of my previous friends, because I knew that of the two of us she was the true Nietzschean, the one who understood better than I did that hilarity is the best response to absurdity. Tell her that we live in the detritus of the Big Bang on some two-bit planet in an undistinguished galaxy—not that I ever put it in quite those words—and she'd roll her eyes and smile as if this tragic circumstance might offer some possibilities for fun. Tell her that we are each individually doomed to death and she might get inspired by an ad on the bus for an attractive and moderately priced cemetery. "It's never too soon to start thinking about these things," she said loudly enough to make our fellow passengers squirm, "and what a reasonable price!" If I could control my giggling, I would respond with a riff into what would happen as the city ran out of space to contain the steady onslaught of the dead. Would it become necessary to start digging up lawns? People looked away and once or twice changed their seats. No one ever joined in.

But she was slippery too, a "phony" was how my mother put it, though my mother was not privy to any actual evidence. If I asked Marina about something she'd told me the week before, she might deny it or say she'd forgotten it or never meant it anyway. She told me with a certain amount of pride that she had fashioned three distinct personalities that she adopted to suit the setting, which was of course one way to beat the "personality tests," but it left me to guess which Marina I was dealing with from one moment to the next—the good schoolgirl, the prankster, or the fledgling young artist. I had been convinced that she was some sort of creative genius until the afternoon she showed me a poem she had written—something about the moon and soft breezes, I think—which, my limited French and Latin suggested, was the same poem, only in English, as the one in the Spanish textbook that lay open on her desk. When I asked her about this, she shrugged in a way meant to make me feel like a dolt for failing to grasp some obvious principle of poetic convergence.

Was it really possible to communicate with anyone—at least about anything important? In that first summer in Los Angeles I reported in my journal:

> It was lunchtime at school. I had been reading, apart from my friends. Then I looked up, saw that the grass was green, the sun was warm, and was happy. I rejoined my friends, who were engaged in the most abstract of discussions, abstract because it was so trivial as to be completely unrelated to reality. [They were probably talking about grades and upcoming tests.] So I spoke. I told them, smiling, that it made no difference, none at all, so be happy. They laughed, not from enlightenment and relief, but from surprise. I looked around at the faces all around and realized again what a wall there is between me and them, them and them.

Or I might be on a bus, studying my fellow passengers for signs of independent conscious existence. "Some read," I noted, "some look out the window, and I look at them. I would like to say, 'Here we are, you people, this time and place and us in it will never be again. Wake up!' But the bus has already moved, and some people have to get off."

What I wanted from people was simple enough. I wanted them to rush up to me and to each other and say, "Oh my God, what is this? What is happening here?" I wanted them to come pouring out of their houses and cars calling out, "Look at this! Just look at this! Do you see what I see? The strange juice rising in the grass and the trees, the great freely given, unearned beneficence of the sun?" In my fantasy some of them would buttonhole strangers for the first serious conversations of their lives. Others would throw their arms out and their heads back and scream at the sky in alternating terror and ecstasy. Passersby would hug. Tears of recognition and amazement would be shed. It would be the end of loneliness and falsity and the beginning, after all these wasted years, of whatever it is we are supposed to be doing here. And if they didn't want to respond so demonstratively, then all I asked was a wink here and there, a carefully folded note. "People," I wrote, "why don't you make some sign?"

I wouldn't have put it this way at the time, but I was becoming Prince Myshkin—a holy fool—though with flashes of Zarathrustra, meaning that my grip on the ordinary was slipping away. I studied, read, kept my clothes clean and ironed, showed up for work on time, first at the TV repair place and later as a waitress. But something was pulling at me, something that now seemed so unstoppable, resounding, and obvious that I was no longer reticent about it in my journal. The episodes of dissociation, which had subsided in the gloom of Lowell, were increasing in both frequency and intensity, meaning that I was again seeing things as they actually were, without, as I wrote, "the superimposed fantasy":

Often I have sudden jolts when the realness of things is lost. Then things are as if I was just born and had never seen them before. It is an adventure [although] I am delighted when the ground I step on turns out to [still] be there and the sunlight doesn't materialize into a clashing noise or stream of liquid.

But now gradually a new philosophical doubt took hold of me. How could I know these glimpses of what seemed to be an underlying reality were "real" when they too were products of my "mental processes"? "My ignorance is unfathomable," I wrote, "infinite. If I sat down, if I was capable of sitting down and doing some logical reasoning, and followed each circular thought, and figured it all out, I would be desperately unhappy. For the truth which comes from logic is bitter. Everything I do or think is mocked cruelly by that which I cannot alter—the fact of my death." Or as I put it somewhat more elegantly a few months later, "This is a difficult time. I am Nietzsche's rope dancer and the rope is imaginary. If I look down for an instant and see that there is nothing there, I'm lost."

When someone wanders so far from the flock, people, in their collective vanity, tend to blame the flock. Anyone who wanders off must have been actively pushed away—by family dysfunction, social disappointment, sexual rejection, whatever. Or maybe it was the wanderer's fault, and, like one of Conrad's characters, she lost her way because she failed to cultivate the appropriate intraspecies bonds; she forgot about love. Either way, the idea is that what happens to people is all about people; no other factors merit consideration. Try telling a therapist or other member of the helping professions that you are menaced by hazy sunlight or that the sumac trees growing like weeds along railroad tracks fill you with dread, and he or she will want to hear accounts of childhood abuse. This is the conceit of psychiatry and unfortunately of so many novels, even some of the best and most riveting ones: that except for the occasional disease or disaster, the only forces shaping our lives are other humans, and that outside of our web of human interactions there is nothing worth looking into.

Of course we are shaped by our mutual dependency, and to a degree that is almost embarrassing. I have no argument with that. Other than certain insects, humans are the most social of animals. Infants who are not cuddled or held die of a syndrome called "failure to thrive." Seemingly successful adults can be driven to depression or suicide by a lover's rejection or an accumulation of professional slights. Which is to say that we are "hive" animals or—to invoke a more extravagant biological metaphor—we are the individual nuclei studded throughout a syncytium of shared protoplasm, utterly dependent on each other for structure and nutrients. To be pinched off from the main body of the community is to risk real damage, and one form the damage can take, I'm willing to concede, is an inability to enter wholeheartedly into what is socially defined as real.

So yes, I was a product of the peculiar dynamics of the tiny group of humans I lived with, and the fact that we moved so often only amplified their impact. As a family, we were designed for frictionless mobility with no competing long-term bonds—to friends, for example, or community institutions—that might have diluted our dependency on one another, as either antagonists or potential allies and sources of approval. And it was clear, a few months into our stay in California, that our little encampment was in a state of advanced disrepair. My father had withdrawn to a point where I had to wonder why he had bothered to bring us along with him from Lowell. Maybe he had already taken up with the secretary who was to become his second wife, because when he was around, he appeared to be in the grip of a vast and terrible thought, leaning on one elbow, smoking and staring off in silence. His withdrawal further tormented my mother, who in turn spread the torment around. But I'd been watching this asymmetric power struggle for as long as I'd been able to take mental notes, and it no longer held any interest for me. What had changed for me with our move to California was not the family dysfunction but the physical environment.

In Los Angeles there just seemed to be less detail per square foot of the visual field. A palm tree is simple, for example, a mere stick figure compared to an oak, and at least from a distance, stucco is featureless compared to shingles or brick. There was nothing on the surfaces that made up my visual field to anchor my attention, and these surfaces were almost always alarmingly bright. Los Angeles gets 329 sunny days a year, compared to Boston's 230, with Boston being an approximation for Lowell. That's ninety-nine more days of photic aggression, of sharp outlines and the harsh planes that made up buildings and roads. There was no hiding here, and none of the false coziness engendered by snow or long days of rain. If something was trying to get to me—not that I thought that anything was—but if something *was* coming at me from a distance, there was no longer much cloud cover to keep it at bay.

"Something"? Up until now I had thought of the dissociative experience as a "place," but since I had no control over my access to it, there was the possibility of some being or agency that swooped down to take me there. If I had no power over the experience, then maybe something else did. But of course there were no candidates to fill such a role. You might say that the major lesson of my upbringing so far was that there was nothing "out there"—no God, no reliable others, and no help coming, or, for that matter, any threats other than those of human invention. So my uncanny "jolts," or sudden fissures in reality, could not represent interventions by some alien being. Rationally speaking, they were nothing more than brief breakdowns of normal perceptual processes, and were ultimately explainable, like everything else, in terms of cellular and molecular interactions. Science confirmed that the universe was dead or at least made up of tiny dead things, mindless particles following their destinies.

Science—straightforward, reductionist, Newtonian high school science—should have kept my feet on the firm ground of communal reality. Or so you might think, because there's no room in it for abnormal perceptions of the kind that can't be shared in a few words or mathematical symbols. In fact, I can imagine science being used as therapy for all sorts of alienation-related psychological disorders. What better way to bring an errant mind back into the fold than to give the patient a stopwatch, a ball, and an inclined plane and tell her she can have lunch as soon as she comes up with something interesting to report? Or send a young romantic off to observe a sunset with the instruction that he is not to come back with some mush about glory and uplift; just stick to wavelengths, temperature, and angles of light. That's what science is about: seeing the exact same things that other people do, finding the units of measurement with which to describe those things, communicating in the fewest and most precise words available. What could be saner—or more sociable—than that?

But science wasn't working out that way for me, and not because I wasn't paying attention. I didn't take the high school course in biology, but I did qualify, on the basis of my grades, for what amounted to some kind of biology aversion therapy. This involved long bus trips to Saturday morning lectures on the subject of taxonomy, meaning the similarities between sketches of different creatures—mostly, as I recall, mollusks, although the vertebrates too were presented as so totally immobilized that they might as well have been encased in shells. Since Darwin went unmentioned, these similarities implied no genealogical connections, and I could see no more reason to focus on the sorting of creatures into species and subspecies than to discuss the way the lecturer arranged items in her chest of drawers. If there was any motion in the realm of "living things" (a fascinatingly oxymoronic notion in itself)—any creeping or running or lunging or reaching—the work of biologists was to replace it with a static series of slides, and this I figured they could do perfectly well without any help from me.

As for high school physics, all it offered was a view from which, as far as I could determine, "matter's chief property is inertia," meaning that the physical world was dead—a huge corpse deposited, for unknown reasons, in the middle of space-time. Let go of a rock and it falls; planets keep tumbling through their orbits; x is always tethered meekly to y. Pendulums swing and water flows downhill. All pretty dull until you reflected on the fact that all this motion arose from something totally occult, a "force" of some kind—which was what? A silent, invisible, odorless manifestation of will, but *whose* will, and what was it striving toward?

Chemistry was a far more potent distraction, my refuge from the barrenness of physics, trigonometry, and family. Maybe because it was the closest thing I could find to my father's erstwhile field or maybe because I was actually good at it—good enough anyway to have won a copy of the *Handbook of Chemistry and Physics* with my name emblazed on its cover for achievement in ninth-grade science—but I couldn't get enough of chemistry. "All I think of is chemistry, chemistry, chemistry," I wrote:

I am a supersaturated solution, I'm a filter paper who's had too much. Chemistry is the last thing I think of at night and at 6:30 AM my first conscious thought is about the occurrence of aluminum. And this is only the introduction to the preface to the beginning of the most elementary chemistry. It's not blood in my veins, it's a colloidal suspension.

Of course if I had really been a science prodigy, I would have been *doing* chemistry and not just reading about it. I would have been like Linus Pauling, who as a high school boy ransacked junkyards to build equipment for his home chemistry lab. I possessed a chemistry set—of the kind that was popular in the fifties and seemingly designed, with its many readily opened vials of toxic materials, to exterminate budding scientists. But it just gathered dust on a shelf, which is probably a good thing, since of course I had no source of water in my bedroom and no way of washing, say, uranium dust off my hands.

I was attracted to chemistry the way some people were attracted to Tolkien, because it offered an alternative world full of drama and intrigue. Physics wanted to squeeze the life out of nature, but chemistry revealed that underneath the calm surface of things there exists a realm exempt from brute gravity, where atoms and molecules are in constant motion, pushing and jostling, dancing and mating—activities acknowledged in first-year physics only as "friction"—the irritating stickiness of things, which to a physicist is a kind of imperfection. But who could resist the erotic lives of atoms and molecules—the violent passion of electrostatic attractions, the comfortable mutuality of covalent bonds, the gentle air kisses of van der Waals forces? The rules governing the couplings and uncouplings of tiny particles seemed to me as fascinating as the kinship rules of what we still called "primitive" societies— with the revulsion of like-charged particles, for example, functioning as a kind of incest taboo. Somehow, out of all this invisible turmoil, the gross material world was supposed to assemble itself, because that's what the world was—*really* was, in a scientific sense—an ever-shifting alliance of particles, a concatenation of unwilled, more or less automatic events.

All of which amounts to an admission that my mind often wandered as I struggled through long problem sets involving, for example, reaction rates and equilibrium constants. And remember that in those days before handheld calculators almost every problem required some recourse to log tables or the tortured algorithm of long division, providing plenty of openings for the kind of useless philosophical digression available to a person who would rather not be scratching out numbers with a pencil, who would rather be reading novels. Science "works," of course, but from an aesthetic point of view, was it really a great improvement over mythology? Why do we insist that theories "work," when they might just as well sit around and look pretty?

I couldn't help observing that for every advance in science—explaining why the seasons change or lightning rips open the sky—some perfectly competent goddess or demiurge is put out of work, a hypothesized spirit dies, or a living thing surrenders its autonomy. Take an amoeba, creeping along a glass slide one pseudopod after another. Do you think it moves because it "wants" to? No, its movements represent chemotaxis—the action of small molecules on its cell membrane, leading to tugs and pulls on the protein scaffolding within, the zipping and unzipping of polymers—and it is this sequence of events that generates the motion. To "understand" the amoeba, in a scientific way, is to turn it into a jerry-rigged contraption that could theoretically be synthesized from reagents in a test tube. Any other interpretation of its motion—say, in terms of "wanting" or desire—would represent the dread crime of "anthropomorphism."

But what was there to do if not science? Science fiction had helped lure me into it, if only because it made science seem like a pure outgrowth of imagination, without any of the drudgery of making measurements and calculating results. Sputnik also played a role, because it meant that from 1957 on, all bright young Americans, even the girls among them, needed to be steered in the direction of rocket-making skills, beginning with physics and chemistry. (At least no teacher ever said, "Wow, you're good. Have you thought of a career in art history?") Then there was my father's irresistible influence—not only his love of science, but his abandonment of it. The sins of the father were visited on the daughter, and if he wasn't going to find the cure for acne or some astounding way of generating electricity out of room-temperature granite, then I was going to have to do it for him. That was the implication of his "sacrifice": The dream of pure science had to be postponed to the next generation, and since neither of my siblings showed the slightest interest, it was I who inherited the obligation.

Besides, as far as I could see, any subject other than science, like history or literature, was just a matter of reading, which I could do on my own. Literature was my default activity—what I did when I wasn't doing anything else and often, to my mother's vexation, even when I was. I could prop up a book to read while I was brushing my teeth or washing the dishes, and there was no reason to stop just because someone entered the room. Reading was entertainment; science was work, and everyone had to work; that was obvious. The alternative was to be like my mother, driven to madness by the pressure of unchanneled energy.

If science had admitted that amoebae could have intentions, that oxygen atoms actually lust after hydrogen atoms, I might have felt a little less lonely. But the purpose of science was to crush any sign of autonomous life, or at least of intention, outside of the scientific observer him- or herself. This was the universe as seen from high school physics class, enriched by rumors of relativity: everything reduced to particles rolling around on the wrinkles of space-time, the billiard table of classical physics augmented by Einstein into some vast funereal topography, like the gently furrowed surface of a sunless sea on the distant planet of a dying star. All of which made the question *why* ever more urgent. Why was there anything at all? Why interrupt the perfection of universal Nothing with the momentary clutter and confusion of Something? If everything else was already dead or determined, how to account for this minuscule perturbation that was conscious human life, or at least my conscious human life? Why, O Lord, didn't you just go right on sleeping?

CHAPTER 5

All, All Alone

About six months into our life in California I began to in-
dulge in a long-running fantasy that I was the only person
left alive on earth, or at least for as far as the eye could see. I woke
up one morning somewhere other than home (in the canonical
version of the fantasy I had had an overnight babysitting job in a
wealthy area like Beverly Hills) and rushed to my car, which was a
nice fantastical touch right there—*my* car—to get somewhere I
was afraid of being late to. Not to worry, the streets were completely empty and the traffic lights were swinging dead on their
nooses. Nothing came out of the car radio. The little plastic flags
strung up around used-car lots still snapped in the breeze, but they
might as well have been Tibetan prayer flags now, cleansed of all
commercial significance. Before I could put together the idea of a
disaster, there was a moment of exultation in the beauty of the
abandoned world. It had always been there, of course—the still-
green mountains to the north, the fountains of bougainvillea
flowing down over walls—but usually hidden under a thick human crust of smog and significations. Now I realized: The city is
mine, the sky is clear, and promise glistens from the world like dew.

I suppose it was the same feeling I might have had if I'd taken over a small plane and managed by sheer trial and error to get it up a thousand feet or so off the ground, before realizing that I had no idea how to fly.

In the fantasy, it takes me less than a day to figure out that all other humans are gone, along with their clothing and ornaments, and without any sign of struggle or coercion. For the sake of convenience, their cars are not left at odd angles blocking the highways, but neatly parked in front of homes, keys still in the ignition. No clue remains to tell me where all the people have gone or been abducted to. I know this sort of situation comes up all the time in science-fiction stories, usually adumbrated by odd lights in the night sky, curious prophecies, and erratic readings on scientific equipment. But there have been no warnings, at least none that registered with me. I had gone to sleep to the sound of nattering obligations—do your homework, iron your uniform, get to your job at the diner on time—and had awakened to perfect freedom.

The first few days, before the food begins to rot in refrigerators, I take this as an opportunity for scouting and some light, abstemious looting. The doors of even the grandest mansions yield to me. I walk from room to room, testing out couches so big they curve around to outline a room, picking up objects and putting them down. So this is what's left when you squeeze the human pulp out of the built and manufactured environment—the chitinous exoskeleton, the wood and fabric system of internal surfaces and props without which we would no doubt sag against the walls or collapse on the floor. Without people around, furniture has nothing to do but bear witness to the structural inadequacies of the human body: How much padding, cushioning, embracing, enfolding, and supporting we had needed just to stumble about through our days!

There is very little among the rich material deposits left by my kind that I want enough to pack into the trunk of my car—a book here and there, some batteries, a can of smoked oysters. Sometimes I pause for an hour or so to read a diary stuffed in the back of a drawer, fascinated by the detailed yearnings and plans that have been so suddenly rendered inoperative. Abandoned pets can be a problem, yipping and demanding food, but there's not much I can do for them beyond hoping they meet their ends as peacefully as the tropical fish now dissolving in their elaborate tanks. I sip crème de menthe, sample chocolates imported from Europe, try lolling on satin sheets.

Then about a week after the disappearance of everyone else, the fantasy acquires a more anxious and compulsive edge. I realize that I have to establish a base. It should be a house with a swimming pool to serve as a cistern, and definitely with a wall around it to keep out the dogs, which, having clawed their way out of their homes, are now beginning to aggregate into packs. The Church of All Religions at first seems like a possibility, because of its wall and freshwater lake, but it offers an insufficient view of the hills, and I need to monitor the entire horizon for any signs of activity. On the other hand, though, my base can't be so high in the hills that I won't be able to haul things up from the stores in the valleys by myself, in a shopping cart if necessary, because at some point my car will run out of gas and the tanks of other cars will empty through evaporation. I have to start stocking my base with canned goods, candles, aspirin, sanitary pads, and whatnot—which means repeated forays into the stores along once-busy streets, smashing windows with a hammer as necessary. The worst are the supermarkets, once so enticingly bright that you never noticed the near absence of windows, but now impenetrably dark a few paces in, after you get past the cash registers, cavelike and stinking of rotting meat.

So what was this—wish fulfillment? Horror movie? Both? I can still summon up the fantasy when I'm in L.A.—gauging distances and altitudes, worrying about the reliability of rainfall—and I realize today that it's a form of entertainment, a serialized adventure movie, which was probably its original function. At some point, when I was probably about ten, I had found out that there are settings in which you are not allowed to read, so you have to develop a mental alternative to books. Things might have been very different, for example, if my mother had not banned reading in cars, which she judged, perhaps rightly, to be conducive to nausea. Maybe I would know more today, and probably would be a more practical person, if I hadn't had all those empty hours in buses and cars to fill with my handcrafted fantasies.

High school was another site of unpredictable reading taboos, which I tried at first to circumvent by concealing my own book inside some useless shell of a civics textbook. When the teacher snatched my book—which was released only after some minor penance performed after class—I realized that I had to become fully self-entertaining. Let them jabber on about the tedious and unnecessary business of checks and balances or the various branches of state and local government. Why did the adults in my life demand so much attention anyway? "Are you *listening*, Barbara?" was one of their favorite inquiries, followed up cleverly by, "Then what did I say?" Sometimes their eyes bulged out so far when they asked these questions that I wondered whether the attention they needed wasn't medical. Or maybe they lacked inner resources and had no way of being sure they existed unless someone like me was around to confirm that they did, moment by moment, with appropriate eye contact and nods. And maybe they were right.

I had wrestled with solipsism, which of course the fantasy was a

dramatization of, for years in my journal. At times it seemed perfectly clear that nothing existed outside of myself: "Oh, the dreadful bitter sense of power to know that this paper, my classmates,
the moon, cease to exist when I turn away from them," I wrote
soon after our move to L.A. "And as far as I'm concerned, they do."
More commonly, though, I oscillated around a kind of benevolent
agnosticism. There was no rock-solid evidence for the existence of
other autonomous, conscious human minds; the people around
me could be projections or hallucinations, not to mention the
sci-fi possibility of ingeniously designed automatons placed on
earth by long-gone extraterrestrials. Nevertheless, in 1959 I announced with some fanfare that

> I have come to the decision, long considered, that I must assume
> as an axiom that other people are like myself. Meaning that they
> are conscious, have ideas, thoughts, hopes, fears, loves, secrets,
> etc. etc. Like me. That sounds absurd but I think very few people
> believe it. In fact the number of people who do believe it is so
> small (I think, from evidence) that it is an important concept.
> Now I know I cannot prove this or ever know for sure, but it
> seems to me that it is essential in any dealings with other people
> to assume it [the consciousness of others]. Not really knowing,
> I can imagine that (1) other people are sensory images only, (2)
> other people are conscious too, or (3) other people are conscious
> and know far more than I do. The third is what I think I should
> feel (I don't know why).

Note the ambivalence of this declaration, from "I must assume"
to "I don't know why." I had not decided that other people fully
existed, I had decided to *believe* that they did, because without this
belief, what basis was there for morality or, as I tended to call it

at the time, "kindness"? Although if you pressed me on the importance of kindness, I would have had to admit it was not much more than an aesthetic preference, with perhaps an element of self-protection: Experience showed that if there was going to be meanness and screaming and hitting among people, I was likely to be one of the ones who got hit.

But at the same time I had absorbed enough Nietzsche to be contemptuous of kindness and the feeling of weakness he saw it arising from. In fact, in some of my harsher bursts of aggressive rationality, I was contemptuous of Nietzsche himself. He looked down on his fellow humans, much as my father did, but neither of them seemed to question the idea that other people existed. As for me, I even doubted the reality of the physical world and the dead or silent objects that filled it. Reality? At any moment it could drain out of the visual field and the soundtrack that went with it, leaving me in that strangeness that lies beyond language. So how could I "believe" in people? And if I were to start down that path, then why not go all the way and believe that the entire show—human and otherwise—represented another conscious entity, a super-being, a God? The ambivalent rejection of solipsism quoted above ended with the statement that this exercise in belief "can only go so far, there is a limit. I will not believe in God because really, intrinsically, I can't prove that anything outside myself exists."

So you can see the attraction of the fantasy, as well as of the solipsism that it grew out of: I didn't need other people, and even if they did exist and think and love and dream, they didn't seem to need anything from me, at least not anything straightforward and comprehensible that I might have been prepared to give. If I felt a tiny spark of mutual attraction to a boy, which was beginning to happen from time to time, and then after a day or two he ignored me altogether—so what? He was gone as far as I was concerned and probably had never really been there in the first place. I kept myself clean—sometimes even indulging in a luxurious splash of Jean Naté after a shower—and I still had the concept of "nice clothes." But the question that seemed to torment so many teenagers, at least in magazines and movies—the question of "what other people think of me"—was way too abstract to pursue. First I would have to imagine their independent subjective minds, meaning that in a sense I would have to *become* them. Then I would have to plant a little objectified Barbara-image within those minds, which would be no small trick. Then I would have to figure out what I, as an independent subjective mind, could do to alter that little image...and so on, mirrors reflecting mirrors.

Maybe I should have kept a few other people alive in the fantasy—a few friends and certainly my little sister—but being able to pick and choose would make me somehow complicit in the general disappearance. So I killed them all, at least in my mind, and I did so without bloodshed or fuss, leaving the classrooms empty, the houses still, the world awaiting exploration.

At the time this did not seem like a great loss, because I had no reason to think that humans were, on average, better company than so-called inanimate objects. I have known people who are duller than trees, as well as individual trees that surpass most people in complexity and character. There are cloud formations that are more riveting than the shifting expressions on an ambivalent lover's face. And if you want a companion whose range goes from gaiety to brooding menace, consider the surface of the sea. As far as I can see, even now, after years of puzzling over the field of cognitive science, there is no clear line between entities to which science attributes mind and those it regards as mindless mechanisms. Not so long ago, for example, before the recent recognition of animal consciousness, scientists were convinced that only humans possessed feelings and minds, and that any attribution of these qualities to animals could be blamed on "projection." But what is mind anyway, how is it distributed throughout the universe, and in what forms of camouflage? Better to start all over again with the basics, I thought—sky, sun, ocean, walls—which were already more than I could handle.

But as the fantasy played out over months, its real lesson was of how deeply dependent I was on my kind. At first I got along fine, spending my days foraging and my nights reading by flashlight. You can live a long time on the leavings of the dead—fossil fuels, which were once the stuff of living things, for example—without ever bothering to think of what it was that died or how long the supply of cadavers will last. As time went on, though, I had to face hard questions like: How long can you count on a battery, or canned goods, or matches? My few quaint areas of practical competence—cooking, cleaning, sewing—had no immediate applications, since I ate from cans and took any clothing I might need from homes or stores. Vacuum cleaners of course no longer ran, nor was there spare water for scrubbing. Now what I needed to know were the mysteries of human technology: How do you change a tire, fix a car, repair a broken gate, make a fire that will last through the night? Maybe all these things had been taught in school while I was secretly reading novels. Or maybe they had been taught only to boys.

If I hadn't killed my mother along with everyone else, finally shut her up once and for all, this would have been her opportunity to say, "See? You always thought you were above it all, and look how useless you've turned out to be." She would have been right. For all that my parents impressed on me the dignity of labor and the wonders of practical ingenuity, I had never fully noticed the huge human mobilization that was required to keep me alive day after day, never pictured the farmworkers, the meatpacking plants, the truck drivers restocking the stores, the store workers restocking the shelves. If you're going to be a solipsist, at least a principled one, you better know a thing or two about subsistence farming and how to put together a simple circuit.

The real blind spot in my actual, pre-apocalyptic life, where water flowed reliably from taps and the refrigerator always held fresh food, was my failure to acknowledge or account in any way for what kept my mind alive. Forget "emotional support," which as far as I know had not yet been invented. What I needed was a steady supply of novels, philosophy, science updates, random shreds of information—and I needed it the way any warm-blooded mammal needs food. And if I was the only indisputably conscious being in the universe, where the hell did I think that all that philosophy and science and fiction was coming from? There is only one reference in the journal to an author as a human being with a life apart from his writings, and that was a mention, drawn from the introduction to one of his books, of Dostoevsky's being condemned to death, dragged in front of the firing squad, and then, inexplicably, allowed to live. This greatly impressed me. But did it lead me to acknowledge Dostoevsky's independent existence as a person, a person with more imagination and depth than myself? And Nietzsche, who for all the bits and pieces I'd read of his, for all the times I'd silently argued with him—did I have any idea who or, to be perfectly rigorous about it, *what* he was?

I cannot easily account for this blind spot today or begin to reconstruct the intricate mental devices with which I tried to fill it. Nietzsche and all my other sources could be nothing more than projections of my own mind or, to put it more impersonally, dust devils that arose within the storm of neuronal firing that was my conscious life. This is what the solipsist is left with: some vast undifferentiated substance containing both the "I" and the "everything else." Maybe there had once been some sort of rupture between the "I" and the rest of it that my quest for "truth" was simply the desire to heal. The characters in novels, for example: After the initial strangeness wore off, it was their *familiarity* that overwhelmed me. I *was* Myshkin, Raskolnikov, Decoud, and probably always had been. Nietzsche at first "really shocked me":

> No dialectics, pseudo-mathematical reasoning, or absurd terms. The tone of his writing is fanatic enthusiasm. I am borne along on his buoyant sentences with some hesitancy and fear, as though I were being misled.

But then I let myself traipse along with him, accepting him as part of my sensory equipment and how the world had to be seen. So maybe there really was nothing "outside" of me and everything I learned was just the confirmation of a preexisting template that had always been there within me or, more accurately, within some universal me-substance.

I wasn't just reading fiction and philosophy at the time, but science, where even I could see that major changes were under way, or actually had been for about thirty years, although rumors or the new "uncertainty" and "indeterminacy" were just catching up with me. First came the news, I don't know exactly where from, that atoms were mostly empty space, meaning that if you kept pressing the table in front of you, eventually the subatomic particles would line up so that your hand would be able to pass right through it. In a sci-fi story, a prisoner, after many bruising attempts, broke out of his cell this way. I can't say I anticipated the insubstantiality of matter as revealed by quantum physics or could even have told you with any confidence what a "quantum" was. But if the "real," material world was a collection of objectively verifiable particles, then I had, in my dissociative episodes, already witnessed its demise first-hand.

I tried at one point to discuss the "new physics" with my father. I should admit now what I could not admit at the time, that the very existence of my father, as well as the rest of my family, constituted an undeniable refutation of my solipsism. I might not have cared all that much about what other people thought of me or even have been able to imagine such thoughts, but I had, at least up to this point, always striven for his approval. This meant I had to be smart and sarcastic, focused on science, and above all a winner at whatever I undertook, whether it was a chess game or an informal contest to see who could make the best angel food cake. When at the end of high school I told him I turned out to be first in my class of more than six hundred students, tied for that honor with a boy, his response was, "So why the hell didn't you beat him?" At which I laughed because this is exactly what I'd known he would say, and all was right with the world. To the extent that I had any notion of a future life and career, it was all shaped by my father: I would be celibate of course, because anything else would be a grave disappointment to him. I would live alone, a veritable nun of science, poring over theoretical treatises until late at night and rising early to plan the day's experiments.

It was a Saturday morning and he was going over some papers at the dining room table, which was also the only communal workspace and the surface where my mother laid out her patterns and sewed, when I slipped into the chair across from him and raised an urgent question about electrons. There must have been some contextual small talk or at least some wily preliminaries on my part. Maybe he asked me how school was going, science in particular, and that provided enough of an opening for me to bring up the odd fact that I had been fretting about for several weeks now: that an electron could be in two places at once. What could that mean? How was one to picture such a thing?

At first this looked like something he could handle. With his right nostril widening toward an incipient sneer, he launched into one of his perorations on woolgathering. That wasn't his exact word, nor did he say "dreamy," but the idea was that science is not about imagining things or trying to picture them in your head. Science is about making measurements, which is a way of collecting numbers that can in turn be fed into equations. Words play very little part in this exercise. Sometimes the results don't make much sense when you try to put them into words, but that doesn't matter because what you're aiming for is predictions, better mousetraps, and so on. Or as the macho physicists would be saying in a decade or so: Shut up and calculate.

Of course he was right. If I couldn't picture an electron, how was I supposed to picture an electron's location? I didn't take this entirely as a putdown, because at some level he was just telling me what he thought I needed to know, should I ever attempt to make my way as an actual scientist: Don't blather about unseen and unseeable things; be a good apprentice; do what you're told. But I couldn't resist the obvious next sally, on the matter of measurements: Can we really trust them? I offered the Heisenberg uncertainty principle or whatever remedial version of it I had absorbed, which no matter how crudely expressed should still have been recognizable to any reader of *Scientific American*. The act of observing changes the thing that is being observed. And what could it mean to measure, say, the location of something that's in two places at once?

Here his face hardened ever so slightly, causing the whole scene to shift from suburban father-daughter conversation to something so stark it could have been lifted from an ancient Greek drama— say, *Oedipus Rex*, only with me in the title role. I know I was not his actual son, only a botched reincarnation in which his magnificent genius mind had been misplaced in a female body, where it was dragged down and eroded by the hormonal tides. I was supposed to be smart, like him, but never as smart as him. I was supposed to ask questions, but only answerable ones that gave him a chance to demonstrate his superior logic and education. The table between us grew wider; all background sounds ceased.

What did I think was going on in laboratories? he demanded impatiently. A bunch of people playing hide-and-seek with things that might or might not be there? Of course an electron or any- thing else is in one place or another, otherwise what are we talking about here? And he didn't mean just him and me talking right there, but the whole business of human communication, collective endeavors, the whole scientific enterprise. If people are going to say any damn thing that pops into their heads, if objects are going to be both here and there, what is the point of talking at all?

Up to this point I hadn't been a smartass, if only because I lacked the intellectual wherewithal for that. What, after all, had I read besides the British physicist Arthur Eddington and a few pop science paperbacks? But I was offended by the implica- tion that quantum mechanics was some soft-minded adolescent reverie of mine, so I reached for the most powerful weapon at hand—Linus Pauling. I knew he was one of my father's scientific heroes; we may even have had one of his books in the house. But Pauling was a *quantum* chemist, I pointed out mercilessly, and from what I could tell, he had done a great deal to advance this shifty new view of electrons. The covalent bonds between carbon atoms, for example: These could not be explained by a physics of hard little particles that dutifully locate themselves in one place or another.

I won, I guess—if it's possible to win a contest in which the father you love or some idealized version of him is destroyed. He turned away from me and stared out of the room toward the living room window, his face blank and his shoulders slumped. This wasn't a dismissal, it was just how he got when he pulled into himself—legs crossed, arms crossed over the topmost leg, eyes as blue and empty as the morning sky.

My mother was right: I loved my father far more than I loved her, and I didn't find out the full extent of it until that blighted day, more than thirty years later, when my siblings and I sprinkled his ashes in some murky Missouri lake near where my brother lived at the time. When the urn was passed to me, as the oldest, to begin the sprinkling, I was ambushed by a sudden rage. The lake was not wide enough or blue enough for him, the Ozarks surrounding it too worn-down and paltry. We should have done this in Montana, where there were crystalline lakes that would have welcomed his gritty residue and mountains sharp enough to direct his soul straight up to the galaxies that had so fascinated him before the Alzheimer's took over. We might as well have been pouring him into a sewer, and this is why I cried—angry at the lake, angry at my dry-eyed brother and sister for imagining that this would be a fitting send-off, and, since I knew he had never given them much reason to love him, angry at myself for crying in front of them.

So what I would like to believe about that Saturday morning conversation when I was sixteen or seventeen is that he knew exactly what I was talking about, knew far better than I, in fact— and that he rejected the dodginess of electrons as a matter of principle in the same way that Einstein rejected the idea of a God who played dice with the universe. Maybe he even accepted quantum mechanics as long as it was cordoned off in the realm of the tiniest things, like some kind of biochemical quirk peculiar to dwarves. But when you started messing with the substantiality of matter and the possibility of reproducible measurements— well, it was not only science that was at stake. The work that had made him a man among men years ago in the mines had been the backbreaking encounter with the hardness of things. When a man swings a pick at a rock, electrons do not dance obligingly out of the way, and however loopy it gets at its far mathematical fringes, science always has to come back to that fact.

The more likely possibility is that he didn't really know what I was talking about. Maybe he just *hadn't kept up*. I don't know what he did at work or in the hours after work when he didn't show up at home, but I was beginning to sense that L.A. held possibilities unknown in Lowell or Butte, and they didn't involve going to lectures on the structure of atoms. Once or twice I had glimpsed the inside of cool, dark lounges where men in suits enjoyed the attentions of the sly-looking women who glided from table to table selling cigarettes from trays attached to their waists. My father seemed at home in these places—Hollywood-handsome, as you could tell from the way people turned to look at him, steady into his fourth martini and ostentatious with tips. Obviously, there were two L.A.s—the pastel suburban one and this other noirish place he liked to retire to. These were not the fancy mahogany-walled restaurants where actual movie stars might be sighted, but they were still many levels of comfort above the scruffy taverns I was used to seeing my parents stop for a drink in. With their perfect twenty-four-hour gloom and soundtracks of recorded crooning, they made the bars of Butte seem like makeshift contrivances to keep out the children and the light. Maybe that's what he was thinking of when he turned away from me at the dining room table that Saturday morning: a nocturnal retreat where a man didn't have to do anything to prove he was smart because he'd already transformed his intelligence into money and could start drinking, if he wanted to, in the middle of the morning.

What I understood, and he may have understood, was that the "new physics" was a mockery of the whole Cartesian, Newtonian edifice of knowledge that both he and I had grown up with, in which one thing inexorably leads to another and nothing is going to leap out and poke you in the eye. If the behavior of the smallest particles was indeterminable, then, in some way that he would also have to admit, everything else was up for grabs too. You could spend your whole life making precise measurements, plugging them into equations, repeating experiments, and never for one moment letting your mind drift toward the unseeable and incommunicable. You could be the most sober, straight-arrow scientist in the world, utterly intent on your work and immune to religion or fiction or whimsy—and still, what you'd finally see at the bottom of it all, in the highest-resolution photomicrograph or telescopic image, was a grinning monkey face staring back at you, the face of your own incurable ignorance, if you like, or the face of something infinitely alien.

Sometime after the conversation with my father, though I cannot say as a result of it, the fantasy took a further turn toward the dire. Practical problems multiplied, leaving me little time to read or contemplate the strange beauty of things-as-they-are. I could not figure out how to drain the pool I intended to capture rainwater in. In another version of the fantasy, I could figure it out, but there wasn't enough rain and the small amounts I collected quickly turned slimy and undrinkable. If I'd had access to one of today's chain drugstores or supermarkets, my life would have been a whole lot easier, thanks to bottled water, "wipes," and freeze-dried food.

But none of those things existed in the fifties, at least at the retail level. As the months went on I became—as any deterministic science could have predicted—grubbier, skinnier, crustier. And what did you do about shit, for example, in the era before plastic bags— just keep digging fresh holes to bury it in or look for a new feces-free compound to occupy?

Then there were the animals, whose presence had not occurred to me when the fantasy first took form. I had imagined that the removal of humans would leave the world empty of jostling and nattering life forms to distract me—an error that can be attributed to the collective solipsism of the human species, which persists in believing itself the only kind of creature worth taking into account. I had enough trouble believing in the conscious existence of my conspecifics; how was I supposed to extend my imagination to lizards and cats? But here they were, and in growing numbers as the human grip on the landscape loosened. I have mentioned the tragic and annoying former pets, some of which, either clinging to the obsolete association between humans and pet food or catching the scent of my canned tuna and meat, gathered outside the walls of my compound at night to howl. Then too, the cessation of the vast and compulsive human project of lawn mowing opened up fresh habitats for snakes and other crawly things, which in turn brought raptors swooping down from the sky. I had to look down to see what I was stepping on and up to see what might be coming down on me with claws outstretched.

And then, a couple of months after the disappearance of people, came the lions. You might think that without humans around, the lions would have plenty of deer to eat in the hills, but they may have been lured into the city by its rich supply of ignorant and defenseless former pets, many of them still fattened on garbage. Some of the new arrivals were indigenous mountain lions, but a spectacular minority of them were maned—escapees from the cages they had been kept in between movie roles. This was my worst childhood fear, going back to the age of about four: that lions would find their way out of Africa or wherever they were and chase me down streets, over hills, and across fields until I fell, as I always would, and became the red on their teeth and claws. The lions could go almost anywhere they wanted in posthuman L.A., and I would glimpse them skulking around supermarkets and other possible sources of carrion. Once I opened the gate in the morning to find a half-eaten puppy outside my gate, its lovable little face still intact, and I had no way of knowing whether this was a warning or, what was almost worse, a lion's idea of my share.

CHAPTER 6

Encounter in Lone Pine

I t seemed like a good idea at the time—celebratory in spirit, since the school year was about to come to an end, and rational in plan. My brother, myself, and a high school friend of mine would go skiing on Mammoth Mountain in Northern California, where the snow had lingered late, and stay with my uncle Dave and his family in Lee Vining near Mono Lake, which is as close to a lunar landscape as you can find on this planet. But as I try to reconstruct the trip today, I find many puzzles in the narrative, extending to the geographical route. Why, for example, stay in Lee Vining, which was about an hour drive north beyond Mammoth? Then there is the greater mystery of why we didn't drive straight back to L.A. after skiing, but instead spent the night in the car and devoted the next day to an eastward loop into Death Valley. Were there no motels in those days, or none that we could afford?

And even if the itinerary made sense on a map, no representation could have prepared me for what was about to happen. I had no idea, when we set out for Mammoth, that my quest was about to come to a shattering climax, which I would spend the rest of my life, or large chunks of it anyway, straining to understand.

Skiing in my family was a completely normal recreation, when available, passed down to me by my father; the women in my family being more likely to favor ice skating. Norwegian miners had brought skiing to Butte, and working-class kids, as well as the mine bosses and their families, kept it going. Evel Knievel, for example, who was raised by a grandmother who happened to be a friend of my own maternal grandmother, had excelled in ski jumping at Butte High and worked as a copper miner before becoming a famous motorcycle daredevil. My father had also learned ski jumping at Butte High, and it was he who taught me to ski when I was about twelve. It wasn't difficult: Get to the top of the hill, either by rope tow or, in the early days, climbing sideways step by step, bend your elbows and your knees, point the skis downhill, then *lean on into it*—and woe to anyone who failed to get out of the way, because swerving or stopping were not among my secure skills.

I imagine that this is more or less how he learned ski jumping at Butte High School—get up, go down, get up again. No special clothes were required in those days; we wore flannel pajama pants under our jeans and layered sweaters under our Windbreakers, since parkas, so far as I know, were not widely available to civilians. Yes, there was an aspect of the suicidal in the way my family approached skiing. But that was part of the attraction, as I wrote in my journal a little before we left Lowell and just after a ski trip to Vermont, though I was embarrassed to mention anything as trivial as a sport in those pages otherwise reserved for the most high-minded speculations:

I have become an ardent devotee of a sport, something unexpected. I love skiing. There is no sport comparable to it, no pastime or entertainment rivals it. In perfect honesty I can say the greatest pleasure (as distinguished perhaps from happiness) I have ever experienced has been while skiing. What I like is the speed and, even more keenly felt, the danger....

It must have been Uncle Dave who suggested the trip, because otherwise, given the available information technologies, I don't see how we could have known that the snow was still deep on Mammoth at the beginning of May. Dave, my mother's only brother, was my favorite of the two surviving uncles, always quick, sarcastic, and teasing. He thought it was hilarious, for example, on one of the occasions my mother and siblings and I drove the seven hours up Lee Vining for a visit, to let me drive his California Highway Patrol car while he sat in the passenger seat, just to see the looks on the faces of other drivers when they noticed that a sixteen-year-old girl with a ponytail had apparently seized state power, or at least one of the state's own cars. All that avuncular jolliness would come to an end a couple of years later when his oldest son, who was about eleven at the time, got swept off in a spring-swollen river and drowned. Dave got mean after that, starting to use words like "nigger" and "spic" to describe the people he stopped on the highway and eventually becoming estranged from his mother, his sisters, and the rest of us.

I brought up the possibility of a skiing trip sometime in April in a conversation with Dick, who was the only one of my little circle of friends who showed any interest in outdoor adventure. He had thrilling stories to tell of road trips and hitchhiking, ranging all the way down to Mexico, undertaken without any adult participation. One day, in a burst of unwonted expansiveness, possibly inspired by the approaching end of the school year and all the associated tests, I mentioned that I had an uncle who lived not too far from Mammoth, and the plan moved on from there. Dick would have to do the driving or most of it, since, whether due to inattention or sloth, I still had only a learner's permit. My parents, or maybe Dick, provided the car, a decrepit black Volkswagen, and my brother came along with us, either enlisted as some sort of chaperone or because he was eager to ski—possibly both. I didn't know Dick well and suppose I could have prevailed on my mother to do the driving, but I was exhilarated by the idea of traveling a long distance on the open road without any grown-ups in the car.

We hadn't gone thirty miles beyond L.A., though, when things began to go wrong. Dick had been excited by the prospect of the trip and still friendly enough when he arrived at our house in the morning. But once we got going he seemed to wrap himself up in some kind of personal rage, as if he were being abducted to a destination he didn't approve of by people he found morally objectionable. If I'd known him better, or if I'd had the confidence and skill, I might have said, "Hey, what's the matter? This was your idea too." But his anger shamed me into silence, suggestive as it was of some sort of intimacy. As far as I had ever been able to determine, anger was the principal emotional bond between husbands and wives and possibly the only thing that held them together. How would they maintain their mutual interest without the daily drama of resentful silences, screaming arguments, and vicious put-downs? But between me and this boy, whom I had never even talked to alone except to plan this trip and who was, after all, a half year behind me in school, anger was shockingly inappropriate and totally mortifying.

So a very short way into the trip I revised my expectations downward from comradely adventure to another long, solitary exercise in endurance. Any anger I felt was directed not at my inscrutable companion, but at Joseph Conrad and all the other novelists who had been urging me to reach out, take a chance, carpe diem, and so forth. I should have stayed home and read

Kafka, whom I'd just discovered in a paperback bookstore and found agreeably disorienting. The pleasures of human company had been exaggerated, I realized, like "only connect," which may suggest something cozy like hand-holding, but should more accurately bring to mind the hazard involved in putting one wet hand on the anode while the other reaches for the cathode.

I dealt with my disappointment by sheer force of mind. I erased Dick. I suspended belief in him. Who knows if any other person really exists? The great advantage of my slippery, on-and-off form of solipsism was that I did not have to live with the burden of other people's inexplicable anger or rejection. During the next few hours I gave myself over to the remorselessly flat, dun-colored Mojave Desert and the familiar question: *What is the point?* I mean, if you tried to put it all together—the imaginary numbers and probably equally imaginary electrons, the mystery of antimatter, my mother's unending frustration, *The Magic Mountain*, my first exposures to rock and roll, and all the other data coming my way—what did you get? Because this is what it would mean to find "the truth"—to discover or fashion a mental vessel capable of containing the whole thing in its entirety, every part of it, every loose end and ephemeral impression. In other words, I was looking at the job of condensing the universe into a form compact enough to fit in my head, maybe as some kind of equation or—who knows?—an unforgettable melody or gorgeously intricate mandala. This was the great challenge before me, to make things small enough to get a grip on, while leaving nothing out.

But the desert stood in the way of this project. It was too big to be compacted down into anything manageable, too smooth and slippery to be stored in words. I wanted to file it under "terrain," for example, and move on to some livelier topic, but whatever category I tried to squeeze it into, the desert just kept leaking out and forcing itself on my attention. Even numbers seemed to evaporate here, because there was nothing around to count. That whole long ride, no one spoke unless it was my brother in the backseat, demanding a restroom or a Coke.

We must have been a pretty surly bunch when we got past the desert and into the mountains and arrived at the confusion of Dave and Gina's little house in Lee Vining. They had three kids then between the ages of about three and nine and, I seem to recall, some dogs. There were hugs for my brother and me and handshakes for Dick. I poured the milk and set the table while Gina fried up burgers or whatever we ate, all crowded around the kitchen table. All this has a certain glow in retrospect, because it was the last time I would see Davy, the oldest of these cousins, alive. There was some talk about the snow on Mammoth, which Dave assured us was still adequately deep despite the late date. Then we went to bed, my brother and Dick on the floor of my male cousins' room, me in the same room as my three-year-old cousin Cathy.

I woke in a sleeping bag to a sense of alarm and the faint scent of urine from Cathy's direction. I knew I should get straight up if I wanted to take a shower before a line formed for the bathroom, because this was to be the big day of skiing, but I was impaled to the floor by the residue of a shocking dream. The dream consisted of a single image: the human brain, my brain in fact, projected onto a screen in what appeared to be a classroom. There it was— the whole thing, the only instrument I had, all that I really was, in fact—a densely corrugated bulb attached to a stem. And this is what I expected to contain the universe in? Just in case the message wasn't clear enough, there was a caption or maybe a voice-over, saying: This is what you are—a sac of tissue enclosed in membrane, a *thing* like anything else.

Ordinarily I was well defended against this kind of insult, which, as I would later come to understand, has been taunting Western thinkers since the rise of science and the alleged "disenchantment" of the world: the idea that all lofty thoughts and noble ambitions aside, we are nothing but of clusters of particles and charges, tissues and cells. This is the crushing downside of science, at least for those who get so bedazzled by it that they lose sight of their own subjective existence. Why should we—the observers and scientists—be different, in any important way, from the objects we observe? It was my intermittent solipsism that generally saved me from the horror of this thought and, at some hard, rational kernel of myself, saves me still. If someone were to come along and say, "You, Barbara, are nothing but a collection of atoms and cells," I would have said, "Fine, but understand that those cells and atoms are themselves nothing but concepts in my mind. And so, for that matter, are you." A solipsist can never be reduced to "nothing but"—"nothing but" atoms or electrons or synaptic firings— because she knows that all these are flickerings of the mind and that she alone is *mind*.

But in my weakened state, exhausted by the daylong effort to levitate out of that tense and silent car and then by a lack of sleep, I could not summon the solipsistic arrogance to refute the dream. And the worst thing about it, which I could not even acknowledge in my journal, is that the dream-brain was pink, not gray, lacking only a fringe of pubic hair to identify it as a probable vulva. So this is what I was—not just a *thing*, an object, an intersection of particles in motion—but a big, dumb, multilobed reproductive apparatus, destined to have babies and die, exactly like everyone else. I had done what the poets and novelists were always urging me to do, I had reached out to another human with some companionable intent, and look what happened. My entire life's quest for "the truth" was probably just another example of what Freud dismissed as "sublimation"—an effort to project base genital longings onto a cosmic screen. What made me imagine that I might ever know the hidden truth behind all things or that such a truth even existed? I lay there watching for stirrings in Cathy's bed, facing the possibility that my parents had been right all along, that what you see is all there is and all you'll ever get. The answer to the question put to me by the Mojave Desert now rang clear: There is no point, so just get up and get dressed and get on with the agenda.

We got to Mammoth Mountain just as the chairlift opened. I don't know about Dick, but neither my brother nor I had ever skied on a serious mountain before, compared to which New England has nothing to offer except what amount to foothills, suitable for the display of fall foliage but offering no life-threatening thrills. Mammoth, in contrast, seemed to erupt right out of the earth, and had in fact been created by a volcanic blowout a mere fifty-seven thousand years ago, which might as well have still been going on, so fiercely were the snow-covered peaks, some of them actually called "minarets," puncturing the deep blue sky all around us. I mostly stuck with my brother, a sturdy enough, self-reliant kid, but who was after all only thirteen, and it seemed wiser to keep him in sight than to spend the last few hours of the day searching for him on unfamiliar trails. Other than this vague sense of sororal responsibility, though, I felt not the slightest connection to my species. The point was to go up and down, up and down, at maximum speed, celebrating and reenacting the violence that had created the mountain in the first place.

It was an unnaturally warm day to be skiing, maybe all the way up to seventy degrees by midafternoon, so we took off our jackets and tied the sleeves around our waists. We couldn't stop, nor was it easy to remember what our lives had been like before we strapped our skis on that morning. Of course the chairlift made stopping unnecessary, returning us again and again to the brink of disaster, the ecstatic liftoff, and then—for minutes on end—the obliteration of everything complicated and demeaning in the perfection of speed and snow. Only when the sun began to sink behind the ridge and the wind got cold did we regroup and think about leaving. The idea, at least as I understood it, was to drive straight back to L.A., arriving in the early hours of the morning.

But we got no farther than the town of Lone Pine, where we parked at the side of the road and spent the night in the car. My brother stretched out in the backseat while Dick and I sat straight upright in the front side by side like two crash test dummies, since the seats in this old car did not recline. No dreams intruded, and no cops knocked on the windows to check on whether we were runaways.

Why did we spend that night in the car? The question is important, because if we had driven straight on to L.A. I would have ended the night in my bed and none of the rest might have happened. I would have gone back to being a normal geeky, alienated adolescent and this book could end right here or dribble off into a standard coming-of-age story, culminating, within a couple of decades, in the coffin of "maturity." For years I filled the gap in the narrative with car troubles: The car must have broken down; we couldn't get it fixed till the morning; we had no money for a motel. The fact that I couldn't remember any details of this supposed car trouble—any sputtering, any towing, any long wait at a service station—I attributed to my lack of interest in all things car-related. But when fifty years later I asked my brother about it, he couldn't remember any mechanical problems either. In fact, one of the few things he could remember was that Dick had impressed our uncle Dave with his knowledge of cars.

It wasn't too easy to track down Dick—the old man Dick, that is—because I hadn't remembered his name right, but I did recall that his mother had been a published writer, and that led me eventually, through the Internet and a book about her, to a voice on the other end of the phone who claimed to remember me, some of our mutual friends in high school, and our trip in 1959. Like my brother, he denied any car trouble and insisted that there was nothing odd, at least not for him as a teenager, about sleeping in a car on the side of the road. He had done so many times during his adventures with other boys, or even slept outdoors on the ground. The problem was, he told me, that I had been overly "sheltered," even for a girl. Before I could muster any sort of protest, he was already off on an old man's tirade on the subject of "young people today," who, though strikingly overindulged, are mostly to be found in violent, drug-dealing gangs.

His remark about my having been "sheltered" may offer a clue about what made Dick so angry almost from the moment we started driving out of L.A. I think something must have happened offstage, just as we were about to set out on the trip, perhaps when I ran back into the house to get something, leaving my father alone for a few minutes with him, and my guess is that what happened is that my father took the opportunity to warn Dick against any attempts at tomfoolery. Why this sudden concern for my virtue from a parent who had up to that moment shown no hesitation about sending two of his children off on an overnight trip with a stranger for the purpose of engaging in a risky sport? My guess is that my father was alarmed by the mere sight of Dick, who was not the scrawny teenager he may have been expecting, but a darkly good-looking young man at least an inch taller than my father. Dick's looks were not lost on me, but I didn't aspire to be his or anyone's girlfriend. If anything, my secret, inadmissible craving was to be a boy like him or at least some sort of gender-free comrade at arms.

In our recent phone call, Dick didn't mention any contact with my father, and, for reasons that will be apparent shortly, our call did not end in a way that was conducive to follow-up questions. But such a scenario is at least consistent with the erratic territorialism my father was later to display when I brought home actual boyfriends from college: Short or ungainly ones were tolerated; big, handsome ones were subjected to tasteless hazing, and almost all of my boyfriends fell in the latter category. I suspect that whatever my father said to Dick had been put in fairly crude terms, with the effect that Dick determined to have nothing to do with me, even in the realm of small talk, despite the fact that I was sharing the front seat with him for hours on end. If this is in fact what happened, then the awful anger and shame that filled that little car, and which were to set the stage for what followed, originated with my father, along with the idea of skiing.

The upshot of this second night of troubled sleep, following on a day of unusual exertion that had, incidentally, included very little to eat, was that I entered the third day of our trip in the kind of condition that the Plains Indians sought in their vision quests— low on blood sugar but high on the stress hormones engendered by sleep deprivation. At the time I had no inner nurse practitioner to tell me it was time for some food and a rest; all I had was an impulse, as soon as the sky began to lighten, to get out of the car and walk. Who it was that quietly closed the car door behind her, so as not to waken the others, is not so easy to pin down: a thin film of cortical alertness, perhaps focused on finding a bathroom, but under that, pretty much nothing. No history, no future, no tiresome Barbara-ness. The desert, the snow, the struggle to subdue my sense of hurt and rejection had emptied me out. And here, no doubt, my many experiences of dissociation finally made themselves useful; a world drained of referents and connotations—the world *as it is*—held no terrors for me.

The town of Lone Pine offered no complexities to explore, and at the time very little even in the way of side streets, so I just headed east to where the sky was lightest. The street I was walking on held a few grudging concessions to commercialism—an auto parts store, for example—but nothing was open and there were no humans or moving cars to be seen. I moved through a haphazard assemblage of surfaces, still gray in the opalescent predawn light. The amazing thing about the world, it struck me then in my radically dissociated state, was that I *could* walk into it. And thanks to my history of dissociation, which had accustomed me to strange and scary places, I was not afraid to go right on into it, one foot in front of the other. In ordinary life, we don't make enough of this three-dimensionality. We don't pause to appreciate the softness of air and the way it parts before us without our having to resort to a machete or shovel. The fact that the world as we find it is permeable and that even slight muscular exertion can lead to sudden changes in scene, as from rounding a corner or climbing a hill—well, we just take it for granted. But on this particular morning I was sufficiently drained of all conventional expectations that it seemed astounding just to be moving forward on my own strength, unimpeded, pulled toward the light.

In the next few minutes, on that empty street, I found whatever I had been looking for since the articulation of my quest, or perhaps, given my mental passivity at the moment, whatever had been looking for me. Here we leave the jurisdiction of language, where nothing is left but the vague gurgles of surrender expressed in words like "ineffable" and "transcendent." For most of the intervening years, my general thought has been: If there are no words for it, then don't say anything about it. Otherwise you risk slopping into "spirituality," which is, in addition to being a crime against reason, of no more interest to other people than your dreams.

But there is one image, handed down over the centuries, that seems to apply, and that is the image of fire, as in the "burning bush." At some point in my predawn walk—not at the top of a hill or the exact moment of sunrise, but in its own good time—the world flamed into life. How else to describe it? There were no visions, no prophetic voices or visits by totemic animals, just this blazing everywhere. Something poured into me and I poured out into it. This was not the passive beatific merger with "the All," as promised by the Eastern mystics. It was a furious encounter with a living substance that was coming at me through all things at once, and one reason for the terrible wordlessness of the experience is that you cannot observe fire really closely without becoming part of it. Whether you start as a twig or a gorgeous tapestry, you will be recruited into the flame and made indistinguishable from the rest of the blaze.

I stopped at some point in front of a secondhand store, transfixed by the blinding glow of the most mundane objects, teacups and toasters. I could not contain it, this onrush: The dream in my uncle's house had been right about that. Nothing could contain it. Everywhere, "inside" and out, the only condition was overflow. "Ecstasy" would be the word for this, but only if you are willing to acknowledge that ecstasy does not occupy the same spectrum as happiness or euphoria, that it participates in the anguish of loss and can resemble an outbreak of violence. At no time did I lose physical control of myself. I may have leaned against a building at some point, but I never fell down. Whatever else was going on—whatever cyclones raged in my brain—the neuromuscular system remained functional throughout.

There is a gap here, a brief period of overload in which no long-term memories were laid down. Somehow I got back to the car, too stunned to feel anything but hunger. In the next scene I can recall we are sitting in a diner eating breakfast. Actually we could afford to buy only one breakfast, which my brother ate while Dick and I each made do with a piece of his toast. I was astonished by the multicolored busyness of the restaurant, the impeccable logic of the menu, the waitress moving purposefully from one table to the other. The mundane was back to its old business of turning out copies of itself—one moment pretty much like the one before it— but anyone could see that the effort was hopeless, that the clunky old reality machine would never work the same way again. I knew that the heavens had opened and poured into me, and I into them, but there was no way to describe it, even to myself. As for trying to tell anyone else, should anyone ask where I had disappeared to at dawn—what would I have said? That I had been savaged by a flock of invisible angels—lifted up in a glorious flutter of irides-cent feathers, then mauled, emptied of all intent and purpose, and pretty much left for dead?

Over breakfast, Dick suddenly became animated. Spreading a map out on the counter, he started making the case for a scenic de-tour into Death Valley on our way south. He had been there before and it was on the way home or near enough, so we might as well go. If he had proposed a tour of the circles of hell, I would have agreed to that too—let the good times roll. We could do anything, as far as I was concerned: Drive over a cliff or just sit in the diner until they asked us to leave. In my post-Damascene moment, these were indistinguishable options.

My memories of the rest of that day, of the things that actually happened, are pretty badly decayed, if they were ever formed in the first place. We drove south, stopping somewhere on the way to use our last couple of dollars on milk shakes, and then turned east into Death Valley, which made the Mojave Desert seem lush by comparison. After a while we turned north onto a rugged dirt road, as if we had a destination. There was a stop now and then when we'd get out of the car and peek down into an abandoned mine shaft or just stumble around in the creosote and dust, flinching against the afternoon sun. Death Valley wasn't only incomprehensibly large, it was actively hostile. Maybe this was just part of the natural evolution of exhaustion, but the insane beauty of the morning had drained completely away, and what remained was not easy to look at. Everything, every rock and shrub, came framed in its own outline of black, like a formal rebuke of heartbreaking severity. I strained to make the dead world burst back into life, but no effort of mine could revive it. Every now and then the mountains to the east would form themselves synesthetically into a line of music, and ever so briefly try to pull me back into their dance, but then they would just as suddenly harden back into indifference. The function of the desert was to cauterize an open wound.

I should have died that day, or—to give it a nice Buddy Holly ring—that should have been the day that I *died*. I don't mean by this that the rest of my life has been a weary slog; far from it. But the story seemed to end here, or at least that was my strong sense for years to come, into my early twenties anyway, when I carried on with the mechanics of living in the jaded spirit of someone who knows she has overstayed her visit: seen all the sights and can find no further way to make herself useful. A girl searches for "the truth." She tries every avenue she can think of—poetry, philosophy, science—all the while remaining open to odd perceptual alterations for whatever clues they may hold. She even wrestles with the question of whether she would want to know it even if the truth turned out to be ugly or in some way ignoble, even if the knowledge ruins her life forever, and decides that, yes, she would want to know. Then one day, apparently selected on the basis of incidental physiological factors like exhaustion and hypoglycemia, the truth arrives in all its blinding glory, but with two conditions attached to it: one, that you can never speak of it, even to yourself, and two, that you can never fully recapture it ever again.

At least those were the terms as I understood them at the time, and if it took years before I questioned them, that was because I saw them as disabilities peculiar to myself rather than as rules that could be challenged like any others. I could not speak of it because I lacked the words, and I could not recapture the experience any more than a burned-out filament could be used to light a fresh bulb. Something had happened, but it seemed to have happened *to* me rather than *for* me or for my edification. Maybe, from some unimaginable vantage point, I had served my purpose, which was to let this nameless force flow through me so that a circuit could be completed and the universe, for a moment anyway, made whole again. Having accomplished that, there was no good reason to go on.

In fact I *should* have died that day, and rather spectacularly, if my old traveling companion Dick is to be believed. Toward the end of my call to him in 2011, when I had begun to make sounds preliminary to sign-off, like "hmm" and "well, then…," he said, in a suddenly energized voice, "I have a secret." He said he meant a secret about our long-ago skiing trip, and asked if I could remember our detour into Death Valley.

Of course I could, I said, trying not to display an unseemly level of interest. Well, there was a reason for that part of our trip, he told me now. He'd been to Death Valley with some friends, about a year before our trip. They'd poked around ghost towns and abandoned mine shafts and come across a box of unexploded dynamite, which they'd left where they found it. Then, at some point during the trip with my brother and me, Dick had fastened on the idea of retrieving the dynamite and taking it home with him. Hence our apparently rambling tour of Death Valley, where he had finally located the treasure, probably while my brother was sleeping in the car and I was lost in a personal existential zone. It was really *old* dynamite, Dick told me with evident pride, so old that some of it was oozing liquid nitroglycerine, which, he didn't have to tell me, is one of the most improbable chemical compounds there is: just the ordinary ingredients of living things—carbon, oxygen, nitrogen, and hydrogen—but bonded together in such an unnaturally painful arrangement that it flies apart at the slightest vibration.

What did he want the dynamite for? I asked, imagining for a moment that I was dealing with some kind of a terrorist. Oh, nothing much, he said. He was just "a dumb kid" who liked to take sticks of dynamite up to the fire road that bounded the city and shoot at them with a shotgun. It was better than fireworks. So that's why we had driven home from the mountains and the desert, on bumpy dirt roads and eventually crowded highways, with a box of unexploded ordnance in the trunk.

This is not an impulse I can claim to understand. Not only am I fairly fastidious about avoiding injury to others, but I'm afraid of loud noises and have been since early childhood, when a popped balloon could ruin a birthday party for me. Which probably explains why the next thing I said was so stunned and lame. Like a social worker who has just realized that the client sitting across from her is not only out of his mind but probably armed, I ventured to Dick that he seemed to have been a little "self-destructive" in his youth, which was stupid because of course *self*-destructiveness was not the issue here. The issue was depraved indifference to the lives of others, in particular those of my brother and myself, not to mention anyone who might have been on the highway at the same times as us or live near the fire roads in the L.A. hills. I had imagined that

I was the consummate teenage solipsist, capable of deleting people at will from my field of consciousness, but he had apparently had no qualms about actually killing them if they happened to be in the way.

However inept and patronizing my remark about being self-destructive, it didn't deserve what came next. He blew up, like the chemical compound under discussion. How dare I attempt to "psychoanalyze" him? Who did I think I was? He hated that kind of talk, he hated Freud (although nothing even vaguely "Freudian" had come up), he hated people who talked that way, people who thought they were better than other people. Now he was even angrier than when he had gone off on "young people today," suggesting that he had been subject to some unwelcome therapeutic interventions in the past, for which I was now taking the heat. There was nothing to do but thank him, in the obligatory, journalistic way, for talking to me, and hang up, grateful for the passage of years and the breadth of the continent that separated us.

At least I found out from that phone call why we had spent the night in the car in Lone Pine. If we had driven straight home from Mammoth we would have passed Death Valley in the dark of night when it would have been impossible to conduct a search. Maybe Dick's entire motivation for going on the trip was to get to Death Valley and the dynamite. Maybe there had been no incident with my father and Dick hadn't been angry at anyone in particular at all; it was just that once he got behind the wheel he saw no reason to keep up the pretense of friendliness. If that was the case, I would have to say I at least admire his determination. I was on a secret mission and he was on a secret mission, and our paths just happened to coincide. My mission was to find the truth, the complete and absolute truth. His was to experience the maximum possible fireworks, even at the risk of being extinguished himself. You don't need any advanced training in the detection of metaphors to see a parallel here.

CHAPTER 7

Breakdown

H ere is where I lose all patience with my younger self. She has come back from the mountains and desert, come back from being whacked by a power greater than herself, maybe even from the kind of epiphany that filled the biblical prophets with their prophecies, and, at least in the journal entry made less than twenty-four hours after her return, she has nothing coherent to say about it. This is the point where intellect should have kicked in, guided by science, inflamed by curiosity. *What exactly happened out there? Has anything like this ever happened to anyone else?* But what we find in that first journal entry after the events in question is an emotional meltdown, unleavened by intellectual curiosity: "I have suffered. I have crossed the shadow line. I have lost my youth. Now I am writing this on purpose so it will look silly to me and not be true." It goes on in this blubbery vein: "The universe has no purpose.... Life is a joke in poor taste of which I am the brunt and which I am also expected to laugh at."

All right, perhaps this is an overly harsh way for an old person to talk about an adolescent's weepy confessions. I hear echoes of my mother here. When I was a little girl she would yell at me for something, and then, as soon as I started to cry, she would yell at me for crying—a crime that quickly superseded the original transgression. An old fight goes on within me between the critical mother-self and the slovenly, needy child-self, whose tendency is always to crouch in a corner and whimper. It's the psychological work of a lifetime to resolve this battle between superego and sodden id, or at least bury it under the floorboards, but when I read that first journal entry from the time I already understood to be "after," as in "before and after," and think of all the questions I have today, I feel like grabbing that useless girl by the shoulders and shaking her myself. *What happened? What exactly went on in your head? Tell me everything even if it sounds crazy.*

But generosity compels me to acknowledge something more than self-pity in that first wretched journal entry: It is, if nothing else, evidence of trauma and possibly damage. Physically, the only damage was the sunburn that turned my face almost black, which was brought on by the sun's UV rays at high altitude, but seemed also to have been emanating from an inch or so underneath my face, where important neural circuitry had been fried to a crisp. In the intervening years, I have formed the impression from my scattered reading that ecstatic states may be something like epileptic seizures, in which large numbers of neurons start firing in synchrony, until key parts of the brain are swept up in a single pattern of activity, an unstoppable cascade of electrical events, beginning at the cellular level and growing to encompass the entire terrain that we experience as "consciousness." Maybe some similar cataclysmic cellular events could account for what I experienced in May.

If there was a family precedent for late adolescent trauma it would have been my great-uncle Johnny, who had come back from World War I with the undefined psychological injury then called "shell shock." I wouldn't make too much of this analogy, because

Uncle Johnny had actually been fired on, and reduced, at age nineteen, to a prematurely old man, barely capable of taking care of himself. He lived in a shack behind my paternal grandparents' house, in silence and isolation, except for trips to the bathroom in the house. I think that the artillery just kept exploding in his head, hour after hour, year after year, and that's why he couldn't make himself heard. I was in far better shape than that in May 1959, of course, but, to be merciful to my younger self, I could no more be expected to launch a rational inquiry into unusual psychic phenomena than Uncle Johnny could have been expected to come home from the war and undertake a study of the Hapsburg Empire.

But then, in another journal entry just two weeks after my return from the trip, I offered a very different interpretation of what had happened. It was not that I had lost something, like "youth," but that I had *found* something there in the mountains that now I could no longer recapture. "Ever since that," I wrote, with "that" serving as a marker for what could not be named,

> I've never known a moment's calm or comfort or happiness. Having once contained all, having once suffered, having once looked about and seen and felt every object completely in its naked and purposeless significance, nothing less will do. No matter how comfortable the circumstance I am nagged by the remembrance of total perception beside which my present awareness is thin and vague.

Maybe I was too stunned to sort things out. Or maybe the experience was inherently unclassifiable under headings like "good" or "bad." What I really needed to know was what, if anything, I was supposed to do next. If I had completed my quest and found "the truth," the moment of complete and radiant comprehension, then there was not much point in hanging around except for the occasional satisfaction provided by a good book or a surprising chemical factoid. And if I could not claim to have completed my quest, since obviously I was unable to report what I had found, then how was I supposed to proceed?

Marina would have been the one to talk to, had it occurred to me to seek human counsel. She would have been familiar with mystical experiences or at least quick to claim one for herself, because when it came to shamanic prowess, there could be no competing with her. Oh yes, she would probably have chortled and said, "That happens to me all the time." And probably nothing would have been better for me at the moment than to be assured that what happened to me was a fairly common experience—if not normal, at least within a recognizable range of abnormal. But Marina had a boyfriend by now, an actual man in his twenties, as it turned out, a graduate student and a surprisingly preppy-looking one, who took up all her evenings and weekends. She was, in other words, going over to the other side, the grown-up side—a place I had vowed to stay out of.

So at this point in my self-education, I had no way of knowing whether any other human being had ever experienced anything similar. All I knew from my reading was that a few other people, beginning with Dostoevsky's epileptic prince, had also experienced things that did not lend themselves to verbal representation and that presumably occupied some alternative realm of being and knowing. Sometime in the spring of 1959 I had found Sartre's *Nausea* in the same paperback bookstore near UCLA where I had first encountered Camus, and felt a thrill of recognition when his hero Roquentin exclaims, "And suddenly, suddenly, the veil is torn away, I have understood, I have *seen*." But Roquentin, or Sartre, is revolted by what he sees behind the veil: "soft monstrous masses, all in disorder—naked, in a frightful, obscene nakedness." He is terrified of the world without words—sickened by it in fact—by its senseless writhings and, in his view, constant reminders of death and decomposition. If his place behind the veil was the same "place" revealed to me through dissociation, I did not want to go anywhere near there with queasy old Sartre as a companion.

I also read, somewhere around this time, Aldous Huxley's *The Doors of Perception*, which was my first literary encounter with an "altered state of mind," and again felt a shock of recognition. He had taken mescaline, in a more or less scientifically supervised setting, and then stared at things like flowers and furniture, reporting that

> what [the] rose and iris and carnation so intensely signified was nothing more, and nothing less, than what they were—a tran-sience that was yet eternal life, a perpetual perishing that was at the same time pure Being, a bundle of minute, unique particulars in which, by some unspeakable and yet self-evident paradox, was to be seen the divine source of all existence.

But it got all weird and gaudy, Huxley's mescaline trip. Flowers breathed, colors pulsated, walls did not always meet at right an-gles. This, I decided, was not about enlightenment but about chemistry—the action of a foreign molecule on certain sites in the brain. During my experience in Lone Pine nothing unnatural or physically impossible had occurred, objects had not moved on their own, and the laws of geometry had remained in force.

When people run up against something inexplicable, transcen-dent, and, most of all, ineffable, they often call it "God," as if that were some sort of explanation. I fell back on this semantic sleight of hand myself once in those first few weeks after the return from Mammoth, and instantly regretted it. My friend David and I were driving in L.A. when he asked me how the skiing trip had gone.

I said something vague and hesitant, which naturally led him to start nosing around more aggressively, until at last, in a spirit of verbal economy, I blurted out, "I saw God." I could see from the wolfish look that came over his face that I had made a terrible mistake, because of course he wanted to know what God was *like*.

This was totally embarrassing, as if I'd been caught in an act of plagiarism or, more precisely, antiquities theft. Why would I want to apply the ancient, well-worn notion of "God" to that force or power or energy I'd encountered in Lone Pine, which bore not the slightest resemblance to anything in the religious iconography I had grown up around? There had been no soulful, long-suffering face, no accompanying cherubs or swooning Madonna—no face at all, in fact. "God," in the prevailing monotheistic sense, is a curious bundle of admirable or at least impressive qualities, including omnipotence and cosmological creativity. As for the most highly advertised property of the Christian—or Jewish or Islamic—God, that he is "good," in fact morally "perfect," I had no evidence of that, either derived from epiphany or more conventional forms of observation.

And what did God mean to David, who was as far as I knew a nonobservant Jewish atheist? Maybe his remote pastoral ancestors had had a sunstruck hallucination they called God, and maybe it even resembled the content of my own epiphany, but I doubted that David was familiar with any such entity or that it lived on in suburban synagogues. I told him I was only kidding, that I was as firm in my atheism as ever.

And that much was true. It was not my beliefs about the existence of a deity that had changed, but the landscape around me, the sensory "given" out of which the world can be imaginatively constructed. The "epiphany," if I may call it that, seemed to be best understood as an explosion, a calamitous natural process like an earthquake or storm, leaving behind it what is known in science fiction as a "rent in the fabric of space-time." Something was broken. Things no longer cohered. Colors did not reliably attach themselves to flowers. Things retained the dark outlines they had first displayed in Death Valley, giving them a lurid, cartoonish quality. The world was becoming increasingly hostile, and still I had to try to make my way around in it.

There was the fight with my brother not long after we returned from the skiing trip, for example, over the volume of the TV. The TV set was in the living room, just outside my bedroom, so if the volume was too high I had no escape from its strident banality, its mocking good cheer. One night I complained that I couldn't read or study. My brother refused to lower the volume, and in fact seemed enraged by my request, so I foolishly marched into the living room and turned the knob myself—leading to a knock-down physical fight in which furniture fell over and a lamp was broken. When my mother got home from wherever she'd been, possibly the community college where she'd started taking classes, she was so infuriated by the mess that she slapped me across the face—me because I was the older child.

I prefer to think that this couldn't have happened. Or rather, like so many other things that summer, it "happened" only in the improbable new dimension I had entered, the hard dry ground of which seemed to nourish the grotesque and extreme. Not long after the fight with my brother, there was a drunken scuffle with Frank, the guitar player. He and Marina and I had gone back to my house after one of his performances because we knew that no one in my family would be coming home that night. There in the refrigerator was my parents' handy pitcher of premixed gin and orange juice—a terrible idea when I think about it now, all that acid and alcohol leaching away at the plastic. But we were thirsty, and, urged on by Frank, I drank until I threw up, then passed out on the couch—waking up in darkness a little later to find him on top of me, trying to get his hand into my pants. Maybe Marina had been through the same thing with him in the other room or maybe she had gone home already. I felt some mild curiosity about where the hand intended to go, but not enough to pursue the question. I pushed him away firmly and repeatedly, using vomit-breath as an additional weapon.

After these two "assaults," I must have picked up on the new spirit of aggression in the air. If the world was getting more dangerous, I would have to get a little more dangerous myself. "Do you know that for the first time I hate someone?" I wrote in my journal. The novelty here was not that I was capable of such a hostile emotion, but that a person I barely knew, and had no reason to even try to imagine as a conscious being, could inspire it in me. He was a regular customer at the new diner I was working at, a low-tipping consumer of coffee refills:

> Suffice it to say that his every feature and mannerism was cleverly designed to arouse my desire to kill. He is bearded, wears an exotic cross, carries a *dressed* white cat, knows everything about anything, and is virtuous at the top of his voice. There are two things which need only to be announced to be destroyed; and they are silence and virtue. It is hard to describe my hate. Just that anytime he talks (about his honorable discharge from the army, his love of all people and animals, his good-christianship, his good citizenship, his prowess with the knife) I start breathing hard, I feel strong and efficient, I stammer, but I know I could do it. Kill him. I hate him. I don't know him.

Ordinarily I might have been sympathetically inclined toward someone so eccentric and needy, but even at an age when I was innocent of political categories other than "communist," the combination of blowhard Christianity and patriotism set my teeth on edge. The cat alone, with its felt-trimmed jacket and tiny cap, made me want to drag this man off his stool and smack him around.

I was a 110-pound girl whose upper body was toned only by tray-carrying, but by the middle of the summer I had developed new powers. I could go all day without eating anything more than a few cookies. I could put out cigarettes in the palm of my hand. On days when I didn't have to work, I took longer and longer walks, from our house down open hills to the beach, then south to the Santa Monica Pier, which was already sinking into seediness, and sometimes farther south all the way to Venice—impressed that I possessed the strength to exhaust myself. Once I got my sister, who was eight at the time, to go with me to the pier, where I sat her down with a cotton candy and told her that she could do anything—*anything*—that anyone could, if only they saw they had the power to do it. Maybe I said this in an overly fanatical way, because she declared she felt queasy and had to go home.

I did at the time seem to have some unusual new abilities. There was—and still is, because I've seen it in recent years—a huge rock, maybe fifty feet high, on a publicly accessible part of the Malibu beachfront. You have to admire rocks, holding out as best they can against all the forces of dissolution, the wind and the sea spray, and I was determined to establish some sort of intimacy with this one. When the chance arose to borrow my mother's car for a few hours, I drove up to Malibu, parked near the rock's base, and started climbing. I had no experience at all and of course no sort of gear, so the only way to ascend was to grip the rock tight on whatever handhold presented itself and hope that the bonds holding together the rock's internal crystalline structure were strong enough to compete with the gravity pulling on my body. One microfissure, one tectonic shift among the planes of atoms, and I would be set loose into the air for a quick flight down to earth.

When I got to the top, or as high as I could go, I seriously debated whether to twist my head around to take in the view that I had earned. This seemed to me the only human thing to do, or the only noble and heroic thing anyway—to see what there was to see even at the risk of death. Maybe the colors would be deeper from this height, maybe I would spot seals out at sea. As for dying, I was confident that after the sudden rush of flight, the end would arrive totally unnoticed. Still, I did not turn and look. For no good reason I can think of, I put my cheek up against the rock for a few seconds, absorbed its cool gray strength, and then let it guide me safely back down again.

My powers had to extend far beyond the physical. It was my job, since there was clearly no one else around to do it, to try to put the broken world back together again. "Yesterday," I wrote, "being deadly tired and disgusted, I decided to be God and be responsible for the whole thing."

I took this responsibility very seriously, as a matter of survival, which of course it was. I had to take the raw materials, whatever they might be—a pile of laundry on the floor, the drone of an airplane, my face reflected in a bus window—and try to figure out whether there was some pattern or arrangement they needed to achieve. This was not a matter of *imposing* a pattern, as a writer or filmmaker might try to do. In fact I understood that it was my duty to "erase" imagination, and with it memory, because they get in the way of perceiving things-as-they-really-are. No matter how disparate or chaotic the data, there is always an emergent pattern, and you know it when you see it because this is where the *beauty* comes in, like an aftershock from the events at Lone Pine. Take the elements of an ordinary moment—a line from a pop melody, a flash of sunlight from a door swinging open, a rush of human motion, the confused on-set of color from a retail display. Let these elements fuse and inter-mingle until something shockingly fresh arises from the mix. "Then make of the instant a beautiful, profound and therefore eternal ex-perience," I wrote, in a gust of adolescent fervor. "That is the Now, the perpendicular instant in the directional flow of events."

But I could not reliably achieve these brief bursts of glory. The morning might go well enough, but in the afternoon there was a good chance that the sunlight would turn rancid and I would glimpse what Sartre had seen—the sneering faces of unnamed, un-managed *things*:

> Wednesday, I think it was, I looked over the edge of the cliff and into the abyss where snakes writhe and devils laugh. Yes really. I felt as if I were slipping deeper and deeper into chaos. I laughed hyster-ically, put out cigarettes in my hand, paced, and wept.

Where was the beauty, then, or even the memory of beauty? I was a failure. I could not fulfill my assigned task and hold the world together. I was too weak, too stupid, and thinking did not help. In fact, I wrote, it made things worse:

> Any profound thought is true because its opposite is true…be-cause any profound thought contains utterly meaningless words, which being meaningless, have all meaning, which is nothing, which is everything, and which door can I take to get out of here?

I had to face the possibility that the "fabric of space-time" was doing just fine—that the problem might be more localized. There could be something wrong with *me*. In August I began for the first time to use the word "madness"—not because I acknowledged any external point of view from which I could be judged that way, but because I just *could not do* this anymore. It was too exhausting to keep building up the world from raw materials only to see it disintegrate again within hours or even minutes, the fragments of sensory data flying off in all directions. Hence my lifelong avoidance of LSD, even when that drug was widely available and eagerly promoted: For some of us, at some times, participation in the dullest, lowest-common-denominator version of "reality" is not compromise or a defeat; it is an achievement.

Of course I always knew there was a way out, an exit door. With a quick and forceful intervention, I could kill myself and thus bring the entire universe to a sudden halt. This is one of the great advantages of solipsism: Someone *else's* death—my darling little freckle-faced sister's, for example, to pick the one person I unreservedly loved—would be tragic, but mine would be incidental, since the death of a solipsist is necessarily the end of the world, and can be experienced only as *nothing*, which is the same as not experienced at all.

One late summer afternoon when a slight haze was making the sunlight even more malicious than usual, I decided to make a dash for the exit. My chemistry set, with its collection of slow poisons, had not accompanied us on our latest move, and the medicine cabinet offered nothing more belligerent than aspirin, but then

I remembered that mother told me once about some plant in the front yard whose berries are poisonous. They all left me alone and I cried to think that so close, so convenient, was the switch to turn it all off with. But there are lots of plants out there. Finally I found some complacent, fruitish globes which might be berries. When I broke one off a thick white pussy fluid oozed out lasciviously. This I tasted. It was unbearably bitter and I couldn't finish the whole thing. Nor could it [finish the whole thing] because here I am.

This was not a serious suicide attempt of course, just a "suicide attempt," undertaken in a spirit of ruefulness and, I will admit now, even a tiny bit of curiosity.

How crazy was I? Over the years the question has arisen again and again, often taking on an edge of maternal concern. When I review the events of that summer as recorded or recalled by memory, I cannot deny a certain amount of symptomatology that it would be terrifying to detect in any child of my own—"self-destructiveness," to fall back on that lame term again, and a level of social detachment that would probably be considered pathological today. I managed to hold on to my waitressing job, but I lost a job as a clerk in a dry goods store because I hid behind displays of fabric whenever a customer approached. I attended the one and only party of my high school career—a Coke-and-potato-chips kind of event at a classmate's home—and spoke to no one at all until my school friend took pity and attempted to draw me out.

As for my one real friend: The last time I can remember seeing Marina she actually broke into tears as she confessed that she'd just had a "miscarriage." Her face, which I had never seen before without a complicitous smile in some stage of development, got all blotchy, and still I could think of nothing to say, not even bothering to ask what a miscarriage was, since I could tell it had something to do with the dark, swampy side of female existence (and was, I now realize, probably not a miscarriage at all but an abortion). It was stunning to think that sex, even with the innocuous fellow in question, could bring a proud girl so low, and my impulse was to get away from her before I was somehow implicated myself. I can't remember how the evening ended, but, even more than getting drunk or risking my life on a rock, this was not good behavior.

I knew something was wrong; otherwise I would never have

used the word "madness" to describe my episodes of self-dissolution. All I knew about "mental illness" came from magazines—*Life*, *Ladies' Home Journal*, and, at this, the pinnacle of my family's upward mobility, the *New Yorker*—and there were very few diagnoses to choose from. Autism and bipolar disease had not yet achieved their current popularity among mental health professionals, and "anxiety," the most common disorder at the time, thanks to the introduction of pharmaceutical tranquilizers, in no way matched my "symptoms." That left "schizophrenia," which in the 1950s had not yet distinguished itself from its terrifyingly archaic-sounding early-twentieth-century progenitor—dementia praecox—in which the mind just crumbled into a pile of moist little particles. As I understood it, other mental illnesses involved inappropriate moods—sadness, fear, etcetera—while only schizophrenia featured a general cognitive deterioration, manifested as a loosening grip on reality. All of my "symptoms," I realized—dissociation and the occasional excursion into mystical grandiosity—could be subsumed under "schizophrenia."

And though I wasn't sophisticated enough to see this at the time, so could just about anybody's symptoms, since "schizophrenia" pretty much boiled down to "abnormal patterns of thought." As a historian of psychiatry observed in 1952, "If anyone were to take the trouble to summarize the descriptions of childhood schizophrenia by various authors in the past fifteen years, they would find every symptom ever occurring in abnormal psychology," and the same could be said of adult and adolescent schizophrenia—labels that could be applied equally well to unhappy housewives and to juvenile delinquents, people who heard voices no one else did and people who ignored the voices of those around them, anyone, in other words, who was confused in any way about what constitutes "reality."

What was different about schizophrenia was that it was *serious* and at the time pretty much a ticket to a lifetime in a locked ward. I would have readily owned up to milder problems like "maladjustment" or "alienation," but I knew that with schizophrenia a line was crossed into the nightmare territory of "psychosis," inhabited by sociopaths and clowns. This was where the psychotherapeutic big guns came out—the shock treatments, lobotomies, involuntary institutionalizations, the antipsychotic drugs that could leave you permanently drooling. If I wanted to live among other people—and my attempt to live alone in the abandoned world of my long-running post-apocalyptic fantasy had not been promising—I would have to dodge any such diagnosis. If only to keep the supply of food and books flowing in, I would have to fake some sort of participation in a human environment that had never really made much sense.

I can say now though, with complete confidence, that I did not have schizophrenia, if it is even a single meaningful disorder you can "have." When I read subjective accounts of schizophrenics' experiences, I am struck by how thickly populated the world of the schizophrenic is: Voices issue from inanimate objects, conspiracies arise among people unknown to you, demons emerge from the darkness. The schizophrenic, and especially the paranoid schizophrenic, imagines conscious beings everywhere, most of them apparently hostile. She makes her way through a landscape so crowded and noisy that she may start gibbering nonsensically herself just to gain some sense of control over the din. And this obviously was not my problem.

Would religion have saved me, if I had one or could have adopted one? Years later, as an adult, I read in one of the women's magazines I wrote for at the time an article that actually dealt with the subject of "mystical experiences." These could be unhealthy, even shattering, the writer averred, unless a person had a religion in which to "house" them. This was the function of religion, in fact—to serve as a safe storage space for the unaccountable and uncanny. You were to carry your mystical experience back from the desert or wherever, and place it on, say, your improvised home altar, along with the images of Ganesh and the Virgin of Guadalupe—a little personal sample of the sacred. Better yet, you'd have a whole church filled with other people who did not find you crazy. And when I read this article, sometime in the 1980s, I thought, *Ah, that's what I needed during my post-epiphany crack-up!* I should have been whisked off to a Buddhist nunnery, or maybe a fourteenth-century order of Beguines, where I could have meditated and discussed the undiscussable with like-minded others. I should have been debriefed by the mother superior—so superior to my own!—and filled my days with simple chores, punctuated by outbursts of group song.

So yes, those last few months in L.A. would have gone much better, from a mental health perspective, if I'd had a religion in which to house the epiphany of May 1959, and a god, preferably a benevolent one who did everything for some ultimately kindly reason. In fact the whole world would be a far better place if everyone subscribed to a belief in a good, just über-being, who punishes malefactors and rewards the pure of heart. Best of all, of course, would be a universe that is actually ruled by such a being, where even cruel or inexplicable things all happen "for a reason." But I doubt if such a universe—one run by a good and kindly god—would bear much resemblance to the one we have, this scene of constant carnage, where black holes crouch in the center of galaxies and feed on stars and planets, where an asteroid could wipe out the earth's most advanced reptiles just as they were beginning to nurture their young and hunt in packs, where babies die every day.

Besides, if I was not ready to attribute consciousness to other humans, how was I going to attribute it to the far dodgier category of "God"? Maybe it's possible to be both a solipsist and a theist; in fact a combination of the two may help explain the long history of religiously motivated persecutions and massacres. But I knew that, outside of fairy tales and religion, there were no gods and no spirits, and I was not prepared to see my experience in May as a possible refutation of that obvious fact. My "epiphany" could not have been an encounter with some other mind or intelligence, because there was no firm evidence that such a thing existed. It was just a mental breakdown, internal to myself, best thought of as a kind of equipment failure.

A few days before my departure for college, I reflected, disjointedly, on the coming transition:

> I am trying to understand the situation. Not The Situation, but the immediate exigency of going away to college. Sometimes I get a grip on one or two wispy filaments, but I cannot hold all the elements of this change at once. Right now mother is in the kitchen crying because my tuition will so painfully drain her resources. That is an element. Daddy looks at me thoughtfully and fancies he understands me and wishes we could talk. Diane is simpler. She wants me to stay or her to go with me. Benny? He has enough to think about without me. The ponderous problems of puberty are his. I am sorry to take so much of their money....Something had to happen though.

I thought I should feel excited, but I knew that anything important that was going to happen to me had already happened, and that the rest of my life was a purely optional excursion. I had been reading Proust, which led to the question of whether anticipation wasn't just a by-product of memory anyway. Was I anticipating the coming years of study and "irresponsibility," as I put it to myself, or was I, through some odd temporal aberration, already looking back on them?

In fact I am very mixed up as to sequences. All we have, truly, is the past. Hope can be constructed only out of fragments of past happiness whose recurrence seems likely (or, at least, advisable). Isn't the aesthetic sense only a delicate selective nostalgia? This week I think Proust was right that beauty occurs when present dim reality is mnemonically connected to some lost past experience.

Clearly I am dodging something here, spinning out speculations to distract myself from something painful. That I was leaving my family, which had always traveled as a unit before? That I had failed in my five-year-long quest for "the truth"? Well, not entirely failed, since I knew *something* that I hadn't known before. But as my mother had said years earlier, after my theological argument with Bernice, if you can't say what you know in words, you don't really know anything. Then I ended this entry on a note of self-mockery, attributing my "spleen" to the late summer haze that had been leaching color out of the sky. "When the weather is better I can be a Nietzschean superlady—becoming, every day, in every way, better and better." The truth was that everything was over—and everything was just beginning.

CHAPTER 8

Anomalous Oscillations

I was saved by institutionalization, medevaced out of the family
home and delivered from my solitary fugue into a crush of new
people. No more smoking alone in my room while pondering the
toxicity of my mother's plants; now I shared cigarettes and giddy
conversations with a few hundred other people who had been similarly plucked out of their natal environments and forced to create
some sort of society among themselves. For a few months anyway,
every hour was densely populated, from my 8 a.m. chemistry class
to midnight bedtime in bunk beds shared with my old high school
friend Kathy, also a freshman, who was so exuberant about our
new freedom from parental oversight that she wanted to gossip
and whoop into the morning or just lie there shouting "Fuck!" because for the first time she could. Think of it as an "intervention"
staged by wise and invisible caretakers: In this institution, most of
the inmates were pretty much like me—former high school misfits
who aspired to knowledge, or, in case that took too much effort, at
least to freedom.

But what really saved me, temporarily anyway, was the simple
meteorology of the situation. I had a choice between Stanford and

Reed, the brand-name eastern schools being deemed too expensive, and chose Reed for its bohemian reputation and its proximity to Mount Hood, where I imagined I would spend all my weekends skiing, or, in other words, reliving the last hours before everything came apart. The other big difference, though it had not entered into my decision, was that Stanford would have left me under the California sun, whereas Portland, the site of Reed, offered only multiple shades of gray—ranging from fog and drizzle to rain and sleet—for the nine months that corresponded to the academic year. Outbreaks of sunshine were unnatural and disturbing, as on that last bright day of the fall when I sat out on the great lawn in a knot of other kids and could see clearly what a foreign place I had come to. Here we were in this Gothic estate at the apparent northern end of the world, where the authorities—because surely there had to be someone in charge—never revealed their faces or their secret reason for bringing us together.

After that the cloud cover came down like a lid, effectively blocking me from sublimating off into otherworldly states. Most recorded mystical experiences, from the prophet Saul to Teilhard de Chardin, seem to take place in deserts in the full light of day. But then what about my ancestors in the fogbound British Isles? Did they have enough sunny cerulean days to ignite their mystical imaginations or were they dependent on alternative light sources like fires at night, and if so, did the relative tameness of firelight affect the nature of what they saw? For whatever reasons, once I was in Portland I no longer dissociated. The grayness, and perhaps especially the perpetual dampness, conferred gravity and mass on all objects, which now had to be taken seriously, as part of a highly organized display. My solipsism persisted, at least to the extent that I still held the power to end the world by extinguishing myself, and this was at many times a comfort. But the mystery of what had happened in May, and the continuation of the quest that led up to it—all that had to be set aside for the urgent practical task of figuring out where I was now and what I was expected to do there. It occurred to me very early on that this was where I lived now, my only food source for months at a time, because outside of designated vacations I would not be welcome back in L.A. nor could I imagine any circumstance desperate enough to make me want to return.

My first plan was to study everything—philosophy and what they called "humanities"—as well as science. But about a week into my first formal course in philosophy I found myself repelled by what struck me as the shameless frivolity of Plato's *Symposium*. Here we were, using up our parents' money at an expensive private college and reading about a group of men discussing whether to drink their wine competitively or at a more measured pace, given that they already had hangovers from the night before. Frivolity did not seem to be a problem for many of my classmates, especially the girls among them, who tended to major in art history, in preparation, I suppose, for a life of museumgoing. For reasons I might have been able to articulate if I'd taken a course in women's studies and knew something about the financial outlook for single women, I had to be more practical. But Reed had eliminated its sole Marxist philosopher in a McCarthyite purge five years before I arrived, so I had no notion of class or economic necessity, and women's studies would not emerge for another decade.

And what was so special about Plato? I knew enough—which was almost nothing, but still enough—to suspect that Plato was so popular and enduring because he was the most obvious proto-Christian among the swarm of pagan philosophers. As far as I could tell, he was the inventor of the idea of the one perfect God— omnipotent, all-knowing, and all good—whom I had also encountered in Saint Augustine. If there was one thing I understood about God, it was that he was not *good*, and if he was good, he was too powerless to deserve our attention. In fact, the idea of a God who is both all-powerful and all good is a logical impossibility—possibly a trap set by ancient polytheists to ensnare weak-minded monotheists like Philo and Augustine, and certainly not worth my time. I transferred out of the philosophy class immediately and replaced it with glassblowing, which was recommended, although not required, for chemistry majors.

I hit college, as it turned out, during the great surge of scientific reductionism that had been unleashed by the "new biology," meaning the discovery of the genetic code and the helical structure of DNA. Why the replacement of Mendelian genes by polynucleotides should be viewed as a "reduction," or any kind of diminishment, remains unclear to me today, since the molecules that had been put in charge of things—with their stacks of resonant rings and long zippers of hydrogen bonds—were as a grand and complex as anything I could imagine. But this was the reigning dogma: Big, visible things were all the products of tiny, invisible things, and although we didn't yet know all the intermediate steps, living things arose seamlessly out of dead chemicals. Hence the hierarchy of the human intellectual edifice: The social sciences were ultimately reducible to biology, which was in turn reducible to chemistry; and the only way to get to the roots of chemistry was through physics. At the core of everything was mathematics, of which philosophy was a clumsy, slow-witted outgrowth. Metaphysics, including the question of *why*, had been abolished or left to the dubious oversight of the arts.

Chemistry seemed like the appropriate starting place for me, if only because I had qualified for a special accelerated first-year course, led by a whimsical young British professor with a habit of punning. "I'm sorry," he would say in response to a titration result, "but you're a bit *off base.*" Near the beginning of the semester he invited all dozen or so of us accelerated students to his house for refreshments and a little "welcome to chemistry" speech, followed by a lengthy hi-fi rendition of recorded whale sounds. Judging from the perplexity on my classmates' faces, this was a brilliant pedagogical intervention, sending the message, *You are completely out of your depth. You don't know shit and you probably never will.*

It was in this elite chemistry class that I got to know Jon, a classmate from New York, who was the first person ever to hit me with an unanswerable moral—or, as I would later learn to say, "political"—challenge: What if I became a chemist and found out that my work was being used by the military for the production of weapons? Well, I wouldn't feel so good about that, I told him—although I have to admit my notion of "the military" had not moved much beyond World War II, minus the bombings of Nagasaki and Hiroshima, which my mother had explained as practically a humanitarian mission, designed to bring an early end to the war. Okay then, Jon asked, what if my work was being used only indirectly to produce instruments of death: Would that be all right? What if this whole lovely institution we found ourselves in, with its gargoyles and fey calligraphy classes, was actually dedicated, at least in the sciences, to producing the technologists of homicide? I found this notion too improbable to entertain, suggesting as it did that the entire panorama of middle-class American life was a façade concealing some fiendish imperialist enterprise. I would become a scientist, advancing the frontier of human knowledge by an angstrom or two, and if any unseen agents lurked in the shadows intending to transform my chemistry into toxicology—well, that was beyond my jurisdiction.

Ignorance is my only excuse for this callousness—that and the fact that I found myself entranced by electron orbitals. In the context of college chemistry, quantum mechanics was not a license to subatomic madness and indeterminacy, but a set of limits and rules: Electrons could be in one orbital or another; they could never be in between. Here, finally, were the rules of engagement governing the frantic couplings and uncouplings of atoms, the secret of how matter shapes itself out of incoherent plasma. Besides, at the time of Jon's interrogation, it was beginning to occur to me, though still only dimly, that it might be possible to inhabit the world I was being prepared for—to do things that other people deemed useful, to have an occupation, to become an actual scientist, and to keep all that was uncanny or unspeakable stuffed out of sight.

In the dim light of the Oregon winter, my youthful quest for "the truth" now looked like a remote and improbable adventure. I resolved to start all over again, humbly accepting as "givens" the data, the theories, the mathematical and physical rules that other, more knowledgeable people had come up with. If I began with electron orbitals, I could build up to atoms and molecules, then macromolecules and, someday, if I had enough time, beyond them to cells and organisms and perhaps all the way to the biological underpinnings of mind. Already, the first-year math course was offering me an example of cosmic vistas emerging out of humble, plodding beginnings. I had had no idea where things were going when the professor introduced us to the Peano postulates, the axioms that govern numbers, or at least positive integers. It all seemed arbitrary and makeshift until, in a sudden moment of glory, the "real line"—all the possible sequential numbers—rolled out like a golden road to infinity. This was the great promise of science, that if you were patient enough, and willing to balance one rock on top of another for as long as it took to build up some height, you would eventually arrive at a place of great order and beauty.

The problem with science, which I had somehow failed to anticipate, was that it involved working in laboratories. Now, I was no klutz, having been taught by my mother to cook and to sew. I could make a flaky piecrust from scratch and install a zipper in a skirt so that it lay perfectly flat. But I had never disassembled a machine or traced the flow of kinetics through an automobile engine, and in the course of my brief career as a scientist, laboratories were becoming intimidatingly capital-intensive—not just Bunsen burners and Rube Goldberg contraptions for the fractionation of liquids, but eventually spectrometers, centrifuges, and bulky instruments to measure the radioactivity in a conveyor belt of test tubes. Everything that was forbidding about science—the tyranny of numbers, the imperative to communicate only in measurements—took architectural form in the laboratory, where scientific asceticism was reinforced by the total absence of decoration and usually also of windows. It would be easy to do something wrong, like waste the chemical sample I had been given to identify, or screw up an expensive machine, or even to do something dangerous. That glassblowing class that I replaced philosophy with earned me a near-failing grade: I was too paralyzed by my fear of compressed gases and acetylene torches to actually blow any glass.

But mostly I just lacked the patience required for lab work. If someone had already determined the elements composing some organic compound, I saw no reason to repeat his or her work. In physics lab, I easily persuaded my stolid male lab partner to do the actual experiments in exchange for my doing the calculations and graphing the results. In organic chemistry, I cheated on identifying compounds by going through the chemical supply room and sniffing everything until I found an olfactory match for my mystery substance. Lab work is highly skilled manual labor, and I had great respect for it, even taking some pride in my deft pipetting. I just didn't feel I had the time for it. At heart I was always an aesthete, going for the breathtaking patterns that can emerge from scattered fragments of data, a predilection that should probably have steered me straight into math. When I hit Galois theory in advanced algebra, I could feel my mind temporarily expanding to contain undulating matrices of numbers larger and more luminous than galaxies.

It was because of math that I fell in love. Well, not only math. I knew Steve, who was already a senior when I met him, through his younger brother, but everyone else on campus knew him too. He was said to be the most brilliant mathematician in the student body, charismatic and devilishly good-looking, with green eyes and a perpetual half-smile signaling innate superiority in every potential endeavor, and I still have a photo to prove it. Oddly enough for Reed, he was also an athlete and a contender for the state squash championship. On top of all that he was cool, though we were not yet in the habit of measuring attractiveness by heat content. He was James Dean rolled up with Isaac Asimov, an aristocrat in jeans and a denim jacket, the owner of the fastest motorcycle on campus. In mythology, the confluence of such attributes generally signals the presence of a god or a demigod, and when Steve appeared one Sunday afternoon in the doorway of the empty classroom I had found to study in, far from the dormitory's din, I felt like one of the maidens of Thebes when the gorgeous Dionysus shows up in town. He announced that he was planning to ride a bicycle from Portland to San Francisco at the end of the semester. Would I like to go with him?

Oh yes, I would follow him, I would follow him anywhere. And I did, on my borrowed French racing bike, up the steepest hills on

the Oregon coast, going well past the point of pain in my uncon-
ditioned calves and quads, sleeping chastely under the open sky,
which often meant in the rain, and getting up to do it all over
again, sometimes going a hundred miles a day, until finally my
knees gave out near Eureka, California, and we hitched a ride to
the Bay Area with a kindly husband-wife truck driver team. One
night before my injury we kissed, for the first time, under a sickle
moon that I could see over Steve's shoulder. Rotate it one way and
you had a bridge or a shelter; turn it upside and you had the horns
of a bull. But our greatest moment of intimacy was mathematically
inspired. We stopped on the side of the road and leaned on our
bikes so Steve could explain to me the transfinite cardinal numbers. These are the ones that measure degrees of infinity, beginning
with aleph-naught, which is the "number" of integers (1, 2, 3, etc.),
and moving on to aleph-one, which measures the infinitely larger
set of all real numbers (there is, after all, an infinite number of
numbers between any two integers). How many of these alephs
could there be? Could there be a class of super-meta-numbers with
which to count *them*? It was in contemplation of these mysteries
that I accepted, with some reluctance, that I had fallen in love.

Love was not on the list of things we ever talked about in the
two years we were together. For me, the on-and-off solipsist, love
did not entail any curiosity about Steve as a separate conscious being with his own history and internal tangles. He was a celestial
light source, that was all, to which I was attracted like a meteor
to a pulsating star. As for his view of human attachments, he was
a self-proclaimed logical positivist who disdained all nonquanti-
tative observations. If I had told him that I loved him, he would
have wanted to know what units of measurement I was using and
whether this condition could be independently verified. This left
nihilism as the only common ground we could coexist on, and a

stripped-down kind of communication limited to sharable data, or discussions of the relative merits of mathematics (beautiful and clean) and chemistry (cluttered and fanciful).

This is how besotted I was: In between the calculus and the physical chemistry and my efforts to learn German (required for science majors) on my own, I wrote him a love poem, which of course I never sent:

> *You in the dictionary of delight*
> *You between youth and years and yet*
> *What words approach without confining?*
>
> *You are this last instant: now*
> *Now: lost instant. You are*
> *The breath before the fragrance*
> *The song thought, the thought unsaid*
> *The word unthought*
> *And yet: You are*
> *Bright safety and brink of chaos.*

When Steve asked me to marry him and transfer to the University of Oregon, where he was now a graduate student, I said yes, although it was months before either of us dared reveal this plan to our families.

I introduced Steve to my parents during the Christmas break of my second year in college, to startling effect. With hindsight I can see that much of what happened was predictable, for example, that my mother would be charmed by Steve and the sweetly quizzical look he gave all new people that he met, the one that seemed to say, "This could be fun." I gloried in my mother's newfound respect for me: I might be of substandard appearance, especially now that I had abandoned lipstick and wore my hair in two thick braids, and sadly deficient in feminine social skills, but I had somehow managed to attract an unquestionably superior male, one as strong and handsome and smart as my father. Nor should it have been a surprise that my father responded to Steve with undisguised hostility and competitiveness. He had been sending me mixed messages ever since I got to college. If I mentioned that I had gone to a party and had a good time, he would warn me not to "make a fool" of myself. If I praised a professor, he would say that professors were all "phonies," incapable of landing more productive jobs. When he learned about the upcoming bike trip with Steve, he had forbidden me to go, leaving my mother to argue that in the modern world young people did things like this and no one thought the worse of them. The age-old family factions were realigning themselves, putting my mother and me, for the first time ever, together on the same team.

The trouble began with my father, apparently inspired by the setting of the sun, challenging Steve to explain why the full moon always rises at exactly the same moment as sunset. Steve must have hesitated or fumbled the answer, because my father, already a couple of screwdrivers on his way toward incoherence, was emboldened to launch a disquisition on the distribution of human intelligence, which he claimed varied "exponentially" from person to person, meaning I suppose that some people are very, very smart and others are as dumb as dirt. But that "exponentially" set Steve off. What did my father mean by that? Steve wanted to know. Was he suggesting that intelligence did not follow a normal bell curve, as do height or weight? That the relevant mathematical function involved exponents? And now I saw my father more completely unmanned than he had been by quantum physics and by someone who could have been a junior version of himself or might have been if Steve had won his muscles in the mines instead of the squash courts.

Then came the part that I had no way of foreseeing. After Steve left—for his parents' home in Long Beach—my father sat me down to explain that Jews never married out of their "race"; they just "used" non-Jewish women and moved on. *Jews?* All along my parents had had friends with surnames like Goldstein and Cohn and Dwork, as did I, without any mention, at any time, of a propensity to violate gentile women. I knew that Steve was Jewish, although of course also an atheist like me, and had even heard his mother refer to me as "the shiksa," as if unaware that I had access to a translator. But in the hierarchy that I had absorbed over the years from my parents, or at least from my mother, Jews were at the top—better educated, more cultured, and of course "cosmopolitan," the very traits my mother aspired to—while Catholics, with their "mumbo-jumbo" religion, formed a slatternly underclass, and Protestants were only slightly less benighted. I asked my father for examples of Jews despoiling women for the sport of it, but he was saved from having to answer by my mother's entrance into the debate. What was he saying? Did he know what he was saying? Couldn't he accept that his daughter had a boyfriend, as most girls eventually did?

Alcohol played a part in the escalation of the fight; at least I can think of no other excuse for my father's behavior, not that alcohol ever performs very well as an excuse. He bellowed that he never wanted to see that "Jewboy" in our home again, leading my mother to tell him to "get the fuck out," and I didn't know which word to be more shocked by. I'd never heard "fuck" from my mother before, and I'd never heard "Jewboy" at all. My father obliged, slamming the door after him and no doubt heading for a dimly lit martini source where he could drink until closing time.

This was the event that set my parents on the fast track to divorce. Within a year and a half, my father would marry his secretary and my mother would establish the hazardous habit of picking up men in bars and bringing them back to the apartment she shared with my siblings. Neither of them ever qualified as a role model, but as far as I was concerned, my mother had won her almost two-decade-long war with my father, who stood revealed as a stupid, drunken, bullying bigot. For the first time in my life, but by no means the last, I was ashamed of him.

After I announced my upcoming wedding—to be performed with no fuss by a justice of the peace—I received a letter from my father's mother saying that it was too bad I had to marry a Jew, but at my age, which was all of nineteen, it was probably the best I could do. At the time I had no idea of anti-Semitism as a wide-spread condition, so this seemed like an etiological breakthrough: My own grandmother was the source of contagion. I pictured her as I had last seen her in Butte, sitting in her favorite chair, as usual, because she was too fat to do much moving around, lost in a reverie about the possibility of making some money by raising chickens in the backyard. Maybe she was secretly soothing herself with the thought that, squalid and limited as her own life turned out to be, she was at least superior to Jews, though I could not imagine what they had done to incur her contempt. The Jews of Butte were mostly shopkeepers, butchers, and tailors, and not rich or overbearing at all. If you wanted someone to resent, it would be the mine owners, and they were Christian to a man. I didn't know it at the time, but when it came to my father and grandmother, the operative slur was "white trash."

I didn't marry Steve, though for reasons that had nothing to do with our ancestral religions. I may be forgetting a lot of details, but our vision of married life seems to have been notably sketchy all along. What would we do for money, since my father was unlikely to subsidize my "shacking up" with a person of dubious ethnicity? And where would we live—in the dank basement apartment that Steve shared with three other math grad students, all as pale as H. G. Wells's Morlocks and morbidly quiet? The one thing that Steve had worked out with some precision is that although still an undergraduate, I would have a place in the University of Oregon's brand-new Institute for Molecular Biology, assisting in their cutting-edge work on t-even phages.

Phages are viruses that prey on bacteria, and their impact on twentieth-century biology could be compared, hyperbolically perhaps, with the impact of animal domestication on Neolithic humans. Here, finally, was an organism far more elegant and minimal than, say, fruit flies or mice—consisting of just a strand or two of nucleic acid coated with the protein it codes for. Life gets no simpler than this: a bit of genetic information and the means to make copies of it, assuming some vulnerable bacteria lie at hand to supply the machinery of protein synthesis. "Life" is of course a misnomer, since viruses, lacking the ability to eat or respire, are officially dead, which is in itself intriguing, showing as it does that the habit of predation can be taken up by clusters of molecules that are in no way alive. But in the University of Oregon laboratory, where I went to meet with my future scientific mentors, phage were just another substance, like the bottles of chemical reagents lining the shelves. They could be produced in bacterial cultures, and their nucleic acid, once extracted, could be fractionated, sequenced, and even attached to foreign genes for the experimental fun of it. Each one of these operations would require racks of sterile glassware, stacks of petri dishes maintained at constant temperature, dozens of carefully labeled test tubes, and elaborate exercises in electrophoresis. As the time for our wedding approached,

I began to see that I would not only be giving up the congenial bohemian enclave that was Reed, but I would be descending to the
status of a lab technician.

It was my grandmother, the anti-Semitic one, who provided the
deal-breaker, and I offer her my posthumous thanks for it now. She
sent me, as a wedding present—the only one I was to receive—an
electric frying pan. The implication was that Steve and I would not
be able to afford a proper stove and would be reduced to cooking
on a kitchen or even a bathroom counter. The prior implication
was even worse—that I would be doing any cooking at all. So here
was the death threat posed by human reproduction, or even marriage as a preliminary to it. I would be forced into domestic service,
or at least a desperate, poverty-stricken variety of it. I sent the frying pan back to my grandmother and told Steve tearfully that I
didn't want to get married or move to Eugene or even continue
to see him on weekends. He took this fairly stoically, for which I
count myself lucky, because he later received a twenty-three-year
prison sentence for the attempted murder of the woman he eventually married, who had, according to the local Eugene newspaper,
made the mistake of asking for a divorce.

Reimmersed in my studies at Reed, I plotted my escape from
chemistry into physics. One reason was that chemistry was becoming less satisfying, more baroque and convoluted with every
passing year. I'd been through the inorganic, organic, and physical
chemistry courses and was facing the dense forest of "natural products" when I decided I had to try to get to the bottom of things,
to the hidden level where matter was interchangeable with energy
and energy could, if so inclined, resolve itself into particles. In
what I can now only describe as a fit of machismo, I bypassed the
first year of physics, went straight to the second, and was then cat-
apulted, with unholy haste, into the occult world of electricity and

magnetism, followed by the austere beauty of classical mechanics. Part of the allure was that the further you advanced in physics, the less likely you were to find yourself imprisoned in a lab, even for a few hours a week. Then there was the fact that I was the only girl in my physics classes, and I reasoned that the farther I got from others of my gender, the less likely I was to end up like my mother.

It was agreed between the chemistry and physics departments that I, their awkward half-breed spawn, would be awarded a degree in something called "chemical physics." The one remaining hurdle was my senior thesis project, which was devised by my beloved classical mechanics professor, the French-born physicist Jean Delord. Who could not love Dr. Delord, a small, wiry man with bright innocent brown eyes and, to round out the mystique, a youth spent involved in the French resistance? In addition to teaching, he consulted at Tektronix, a local company that made oscilloscopes and other equipment, and it was no doubt there that he came up with my senior thesis project. Someone had to measure "semiconductor effects on the corrosion of silicon," as my thesis stated the project's initial purpose, an undertaking just dull and routine enough for a reliable but hardly brilliant student like me. My father was impressed that I was finally about to contribute to the nation's great scientific-industrial enterprise.

But I didn't. Delord helped me set up a little lab in what I recall as an isolated spot at the end of a dark corridor, in a building far removed from classrooms or any other form of human traffic. I had an electrometer from the physics department and a shelf full of reagents supplied by the chemistry department—my own tiny world to dominate. The expectation, as in any experiment, was that at any level of current there should be a single value of voltage to record. No freakish surprises, such as might occur while observing aggressive behavior within a troop of wild baboons, were expected, because what you hope to find in a lab is nature at its most submissive, ready to give up its secrets on command. But as I reported in my thesis, things went wrong from the start. I could not get just one value to record. "The electrode potential of 0.2 ohm-cm. p-type Si never attained a steady value," and "attempts to eliminate the disturbing influence failed." In a certain ranges of voltages, instead of giving me a single number to record in my notebook, "the Si potential continued to oscillate with the regularity and persistency of an AC current."

Naturally the first suspect was dirt, though it was hard to imagine how a speck of foreign matter could produce such neat and orderly results. I dismantled my apparatus, replaced the polyethylene beaker that my electrodes were suspended in, scrubbed everything, and tried again. The oscillations continued as before, and repeated this idiosyncratic behavior the next day for Delord, who, suspecting "noise," the electronic equivalent of dirt, was moved to get me a new potentiometer to replace the old electrometer, as well as a fresh supply of electrodes from Tektronix. Nothing helped. I worked late into the night, sustained by black instant coffee and Lorna Doone cookies from the snack dispenser down the corridor—adjusting one thing after another, recalibrating, recleaning—but still the system refused to cooperate. The lovely regular sinelike waves kept coming, but from what? I had to suppress the dangerously heretical thought that I was not alone in my lab.

You see, in a laboratory the objects of interest are supposed to be dead, as they are in a morgue, or at least very near death at the time of their arrival. I learned this in the years of lab work that, sadly enough, ended up as my graduate studies in cellular and molecular biology. If you want to study cells, you have to kill them first—scrape them onto a microscope slide and "fix" them in formaldehyde. In general, the study of life usually begins with violent death, or as scientists call it, "sacrifice." Alexander the Great is said to have begun each day with the public sacrifice of a goat or a sheep, and in the research that finally led to my Ph.D., I started each day's work with the murder of about a dozen white mice. Holding the mouse by the tail with tweezers, I plunged it into a jar containing formaldehyde-soaked cotton batting, then pinned it down face-up with a tack through each paw, so I could cut open its belly, clamp back the skin, and remove a syringe-full of peritoneal fluid from the still-living creature. I, the Dr. Mengele of the mouse world, killed approximately twelve hundred mice this way, in the service of an education I never made any occupational use of.

So of course I was alone in my little chemical physics lab at Reed, the peculiar voltage oscillations notwithstanding. If experimental biology begins with killing, physics, as I had concluded in high school, rules out all life from the start. I'm not just talking about Newtonian "inertia," the property that prevents inorganic matter from going anywhere on its own. There is the, from my point of view, even more formidable second law of thermodynamics, which says that, at least in a "closed system," everything tends toward death, or toward rot, or at least toward extreme boringness. Add a few drops of red liquid to a beaker of water and the intricate swirls of color will quickly dissipate into a homogeneous pink. Let the universe run its course and it will eventually arrive at state of uniform "heat death," without stars or planets or of course astronomers to observe them. Entropy can only increase; order cannot arise out of disorder; patterns do not emerge out of formlessness. And if electrons have to get from one electrode to another, they're going to take the shortest route, without breaking out into some ritual of rhythmic swaying on the way, as my voltage readings seemed to suggest.

Dr. Delord's disappointment was obvious. I had been given a simple, even conceptually simple-minded task and had failed spectacularly. One of his classical mechanics lectures had begun with the electrifying words, "Take the sun…," and I had felt for a moment as if that burning orb had been passed directly to me. Now I had dropped it. He alone could testify that I had done nothing wrong. He had supplied my equipment and materials; he had run the experiment himself and I had seen his shoulders slump when he generated the same bizarrely lifelike results as I had. But the bottom line was that Tektronix would not get the straightforward data it was expecting, and I had no "thesis" to advance, which meant that I might not graduate and move on, as in the normal course of human development, to graduate school.

It was almost April and time was running out. My life contracted into the confines of my lab, where for a while I tried to reassert control by determining what factors, such as temperature and the concentration of hydrofluoric acid, affected the frequency and amplitude of the oscillations. But no consistent patterns emerged. I was in charge in only one way: I controlled the switch that supplied the power that set the whole ungovernable chain of events into action. When I decided to bike home at the end of the evening, through the rain and fog of a Portland night, that was it: The party was over. Other than that, though, the oscillations kept recurring—sometimes neat and sinusoidal, sometimes spiky and irregular. Of course nothing in my little circuit "wanted" anything, but the persistent oscillations invited a kind of anthropomorphism: Something was mocking me. I began to look at my smooth-faced electrodes with fear and the beginnings of anger.

How would you like it, fuckers, if I gave you a bath in pure hydrofluoric acid?

When the time came to write up my results, such as they were, only a few weeks before the deadline, I made a cool assessment of the situation, then went to the chemical supply room and ordered a jar of reagent-grade Dexedrine, which as far as I knew was perfectly legal. I'd had very few experiences of psychoactive drugs, which were just beginning to show up on campus, but my one prior use of a drug as a study aid had been brilliantly successful. A few months earlier I had taken a Ritalin pill the afternoon before an oral exam in organic chemistry and stayed up all night rereading the textbook, right down to the footnotes, in a state of obsessive fascination, with the result that I dazzled the organic chemistry professor, whose enthusiastic recommendation helped earn me admission to the elite graduate school of my choice.

I didn't know exactly what Dexedrine would do, but I was pretty sure the effects did not include sleep, which I calculated I had no more time for. The initial surge of the drug empowered me to fill page after page with differential equations and graphs linking current, impedance, and concentrations of reagents, desperate to see some new pattern emerge. But about forty-eight hours into sleep deprivation, the waves of oscillations in my graphs began to take liquid form and carry me out into a dark and infinite sea. Maybe this was just too deep for me and I would never make my way out. Dexedrine offers no hallucinations or, as far as I can tell, any insights of either the mystical or rational variety. But it did occur to me again, as the sky lightened on the third morning of sleeplessness, that maybe I had *not* been alone in the lab. I could have been up against some sort of living antagonist, a low-level demiurge concerned with protecting the surface of semiconductors from the etchings and other torments inflicted by humans.

It is striking, when I look back on it, how much my experiments, with their acid baths and jolts of current, resembled contemporary forms of torture. The information I wanted to extract was simple enough, something like, "The effect of corrosion on the silicon electrode was found to be...," which could then be further condensed to "Barbara Alexander has completed her thesis requirement..."

Or maybe I had encountered something higher up in the chain of command than an ordinary demiurge, something that was attempting to communicate with me through the voltage tracings, if only I could make out the message. What if it was the same Other, or at least the same category of entity, that I had encountered in the mountains and desert almost exactly four years earlier?

But that would be crazy—worse than crazy, it would be paranoid. What was I imagining—that I was being *pursued*? I had decided shortly after Lone Pine that there was no Other to encounter, that what had happened in the mountains was a process occurring entirely within my own mind, meaning brain, and eventually explainable in terms of observable activities at the cellular level, such as the synchronization of neuronal firing patterns and sudden "avalanches" of neural activity. So too the much simpler silicon electrode could be forced to give up its secrets, because it is the business of science to crush all forms of alien intention and replace them with predictable mechanisms.

Upping the dose of Dexedrine barely allowed me to tread water, with the result that as soon as I turned in my thesis, I collapsed, turned blue, and became too breathless to ride my bike. Medical attention was certainly warranted, but I just drank a couple of beers with my housemate, who had participated in the Dexedrine orgy with me, and fell into a fourteen-hour sleep. If I can no longer understand my thesis today, entitled "Electrochemical Oscillations at the Silicon Anode" and kindly shipped to me by Reed College, it may not only be because I have forgotten calculus and electrochemistry. I suspect that a deep, churning, chemically induced incoherence runs through it.

Dr. Delord accepted the draft of my thesis, thus allowing me to graduate, but only on the condition that I spend part of my summer in the superior technical libraries of New York City, where my graduate school was located, trying to find a few more precedents than the rather diffident and inconclusive ones I had so far collected. It would be impossible, in the view of the physics faculty, to report something completely anomalous that had never been observed before. The universe does not reveal itself to undergraduates or fools: This is the entire premise of higher education. So if I had seen waves, someone before me, older and suitably credentialed, must at least have seen a few ripples. In the hierarchical world of science, the young have little to offer except their obeisance.

Thanks to the 42nd Street New York Public Library, with its deep archives of foreign and early-twentieth-century scientific journals, I did find a few more precedents, both for oscillations at the silicon electrode and for "anomalous," lifelike chemical reactions in general. At that particular time, the consensus among the small number of chemists who had looked into these matters seemed to be that the voltage oscillations corresponded to the formation and subsequent dissolution of an oxide film on the silicon electrode, although the reason for the oscillations, as opposed to normal, continuously flowing chemical reactions, remained unclear. Still, I was by no means exonerated. When I told my father about the oxide film theory, he snorted that the only thing I had "discovered" in my research was a "dirty electrode," which left me feeling that I was the source of pollution after all. For decades, I tried to put that thesis out of my mind, as if it had been a bout of public incontinence or some similar occasion of shame.

Only now, after fifty years of denial followed by a few weeks of intense research into the mystery of the silicon electrode, can I declare myself finally redeemed. Everything happened as I reported it. There had been no "dirt" or "noise" beyond the normal smudginess of the physical world. The problem was that in 1963 there was no theory to explain phenomena like this, in which dead matter seems to organize itself into unexpected patterns. Nor could I have known about the martyrdom of the Soviet chemist Boris Belousov, who in 1951 had stumbled upon a similarly anomalous finding, one involving a chemical reaction that produced regular oscillations in the color of his reagents. When he submitted a paper on this phenomenon to a peer-reviewed chemical journal, it was rejected as "impossible" and in violation of the second law of thermodynamics. After a number of further attempts at publication were also rejected, Belousov, thoroughly humiliated, abandoned science. It was not until 1980, ten years after his death, that his work, after repeated replications in other laboratories, received a prestigious Lenin Prize.

At the time of my own mysterious finding, a theory was just beginning to germinate, bubbling up more from mathematics than the physics, but it would be at least another decade before any equations existed to describe the sort of thing I had observed, and they would turn out to be totally unlike any equations I had ever seen. In fact, they are not even "equations," they are called algorithms or "maps," and they offer no definite predictions, just a sense of how things unfold from one point or set of conditions to the next. An equation is static and can be mistaken for a tautology, but an algorithm is a recipe for motion and growth. I am in no way qualified to describe this new science of "nonlinear dynamics" or, as it is sometimes more sensationally termed, "chaos theory," but more and more so-called complex phenomena, like weather and even the onset of epileptic seizures, have been yielding to this new mode of explanation. All I really understand, from my limited reading, is that nonlinear dynamics represents a paradigm shift at least as shocking as quantum mechanics. Which is not the kind of thing you want to encounter when you're just trying to finish up your senior year of college.

As of this writing, I have accumulated a number of articles on the odd behavior of silicon electrodes and managed to read in most cases at least the "abstract," "discussion," and "conclusion." My father, who for obvious career reasons took an active interest in semiconductors like silicon, would have been fascinated by the chemistry. As far as I can make out, the storyline centers on microscopic pores that form on the eroding silicon surface—veritable catnip for a metallurgist. But from there on the math gets funky and the story takes a nonlinear twist: The pores generate "bursts" of current that somehow manage to synchronize with each other to create a macroscopically observable "self-organized process." If my father had scoffed at quantum mechanics, I'm afraid he would have sneered at nonlinear dynamics, especially if accompanied by the notion of "chaos." He would have concluded that science, with its newfound attachment to "uncertainty" and "probability," had grown weak at the knees and unable to take a stand against the unknown. I suspect he would have seen the entire twentieth-century progression—quantum mechanics, then nonlinear dynamics—as part of a long, tragic slide toward decadence and mysticism.

And considering the silliness that chronically infects the interface between science and popular culture, he might have been justified. Whenever a crack appears in the lockstep logic of cause and effect—from *this* to *that*—a certain kind of opportunist sees openings for boundless free will, or even God. We can skip right by the tedium of math and science and admit that anything, anything can happen in this magical universe we inhabit: Particles can communicate across galaxies, wishes can be fulfilled through "visualization," diseases can be vanquished by "positive thoughts." Whee!

But it's true—and I wish my father was alive and lucid enough to discuss this—that the reductionist core of the old science has been breached. We have had to abandon a model of the universe in which tiny hard particles interact and collide to produce, through a series of ineluctable, irreversible steps, the macroscopic world as we know it. The heartbreakingly dead landscape of physics, which I had first encountered in high school, has come squirming into a kind of "life." But there is no way I could have known this when I was twenty-one, nor would I have had any idea of what to do with the information if I had.

CHAPTER 9

Suicide and Guilt

M y mother's first suicide attempt, in early September 1964, barely grazed me, which is to say that I successfully fended it off. I didn't give much thought at this point to other people's emotional states, except as a subject for theoretical speculation, and least of all hers, probably since I'd expended so much of my childhood energy trying to avoid being sucked into her personal vortex of anger and disappointment. I might have told you that there were other, far more vivid things going on in my new life as a graduate student in New York City, things that distracted me from the spectacle of her decline, and there were, but insofar as I can identify my own feelings at the time, I just didn't care. The literary precedent, although it didn't occur to me then, is *The Stranger* by Camus, which opens with the lines, "Mother died today. Or maybe yesterday; I can't be sure."

In high school I had fretted over the possibility that I was mentally ill, but in the wake of my mother's near-drowning experience, I faced a less flattering diagnosis—that I was selfish and mean. It was my mother's sister Jean who articulated the accusation, calling to tell me that my mother had just survived a suicide attempt, and where had I been when she needed me? Apparently my mother had loaded up on alcohol and sleeping pills before walking off a pier at Atlantic City, where she had been an alternate delegate at the Democratic convention, but had flailed around in the water enough to be noticed and rescued. She had repeatedly tried to call me before attempting to take her own life, according to Jean, who had once loved me enough to name one of her daughters after me, and was now yelling at me over the phone about the moist, smothering concept of "responsibility." I was horrified, although not on account of my mother, I am sorry to say, but because I had discovered in Jean a vantage point from which I was not a bold existential seeker—just, as my mother had so often suggested, a cold, aloof person, unfit for human company.

Jean's tirade rested on the assumption that I would have dissuaded my mother from trying to kill herself, but anyone could see that she was spiraling toward ruin in one form or another. She had gotten no alimony or settlement of any kind from the divorce, either because she was too proud or inept to fight for it or because there never really was much money there, just the illusion of wealth created by my father's expense account. So she was working at various retail jobs while trying halfheartedly to keep my teenage brother and sister out of trouble. She was also drinking recklessly and bringing men home from bars, to the dismay of my little sister.

Sometime in early 1964, she and my siblings had decamped from L.A. to Ames, Iowa, for the putative support offered by her sister and her mother (the latter having moved from Butte to Ames when Jean went through her own breakdown a few years earlier and became temporarily unable to take care of her children). The move to Iowa soon led to tensions between my mother and Jean—my favorite aunt, the one who had taught me how to smoke cigarettes a few years earlier—because I suspect Jean was embarrassed to have anyone as risqué as a "divorcée" sloshing into her respectable life. Jean's husband was a doctor, a Republican, an Episcopalian, and a collector of Civil War memorabilia, while my mother, with her drinking and atheism, was almost bohemian by Ames's standards, intolerant and mercurial, once even getting drunk at a social gathering and picking a theological fight with the Episcopalian minister. In the early summer of 1964 she cut her child-raising responsibilities in half by sending my thirteen-year-old sister back to L.A. to be raised by my father and his second wife: a move that replicated her own abandonment as a child, not perfectly, but near enough.

On my occasional visits to Ames, I was expected to participate in the new ritual she had developed since her divorce. She had always liked to smoke and drink and talk into the evening, and now she did so compulsively, with minimal encouragement, as single-mindedly as a solitary writer sitting down to fill a blank page. In fact I think this was her equivalent of writing, or at least her way of organizing a narrative out of the scraps. After the dinner dishes had been put away, she poured us drinks—"highballs," they were called, meaning possibly "Seven and Sevens"—and sat me down for a nonstop monologue on themes of her selection. It was gratifying, in a way, to be treated as an equal and offered my own ashtray and drink, or at least restored to my early childhood role as confidante, but I would find the next morning that I had no memory of what she had said. The plots were too tangled, the personae too similar, the undertone of resentment too uniform. One theme I can recall had to do with people who had slighted her in some way or seemed to look down on her, and there were a lot of people in that category, if only because she didn't have a college education, and now not even a husband or house of her own. But then these people always turned out to be shallow and ignorant themselves, as evidenced, for example, by the complete absence of books in their homes. Or she would retrace the narrative of her own sad existence, from her lonely childhood with her grandparents to her betrayal by my father, always ending in sodden despair, because although she couldn't expect me to understand this, given how "above it all" I always pretended to be, a woman is nothing without a man.

Eventually these monologues got her in trouble, or at least a tiny, small-town version of trouble. She befriended a young woman in Ames, whom, like me, she plied with liquor and recruited as an audience. But this woman, who may have been a graduate student in English, I can't remember, turned out to be a traitor and a spy. A few weeks into their apparent friendship, she published a barely disguised story of my family in some, needless to say, obscure local literary magazine, and there it all was, not elegantly written but faithfully rendered: the heroic rise out of Butte, the scramble for material comfort, the decline into adultery and, though it was perfectly evident without being mentioned by name, alcoholism. It made a good story in the *American Tragedy* vein, with its arc of success and disillusionment, but it was all too recognizable, including to some friends of Jean's. My mother processed her humiliation by incorporating the story of the story into her monologues as one more example of betrayal and occasion for bitter tears. Two or three hours into one of these sessions and I would have to fight the impulse to say: You can stop right here. There's no need for any of this to continue.

So it may be just as well that my mother couldn't reach me when she was on the verge of killing herself, because if she had gotten maudlin over the phone, as she almost surely would have, I might have told her that there are situations in which suicide is the most rational choice and that I could certainly understand. The reason she *couldn't* reach me is so bizarre that I didn't even try to tell Jean. For reasons connected to my increasing distaste for lab work, I had spent the last few weeks of the summer in Istanbul—the period when my mother was in Atlantic City—attending an international summer school in quantum chemistry, with no regular access to a phone.

Why quantum chemistry in Istanbul? Well, almost a year earlier, in some kind of spasm of hubris and denial, I had presented myself at Rockefeller University in New York as a graduate student in its fledgling theoretical physics department. At the time I had my reasons: I was still trying to get to the bottom of things, to the reductionist roots from which all phenomena arise, and furthermore I knew that unless Rockefeller acquired a linear accelerator, there would be no possibility of laboratory work, because most of what went on in this physics department concerned subatomic particles. But I realized at some level that this choice of subject matter was insane, like taking up a career as a novelist, only in Chinese.

I spent the first few months of graduate school pretending to be a student of theoretical physics. This required no great acting skill beyond the effort to appear unperturbed in the face of the inexplicable, which is as far as I can see one of the central tasks of adulthood. But it didn't take long before I admitted defeat. In college I had gone from chemistry to physics, moving purposefully, I felt, from the complicated to the ever more fundamental, from the macro to the micro and below that to the nano and pico. Throughout my education I had always managed to make up for a sketchy background through heroic bouts of study, but this didn't work when the subject was "strangeness" or the fundamental symmetries of nature. I realized that if I was going to continue as a graduate student at all, and thus continue to receive my fellowship, I would have to reverse course and ascend the ladder of complexity all the way up to biology, which was after all Rockefeller's central area of endeavor. I would not go as far as organisms, I promised myself, and their baroque proliferation of strategies and shapes; I would stick as close as I could to the clean edges of chemistry.

The organization of lab work was, and still is, entirely feudal. A "lab" was not only a place or a room or series of rooms, it was the fiefdom of a particular scientist. To "go into" a lab as a grad student was to apprentice yourself to this scientist, with the idea that you would, after several years of patient toil, ascend to a similar rank yourself, at which point you would be able to offload the manual labor to people more junior than yourself. After escaping from physics, I was snatched up by a rising member of the scientific bourgeoisie, the immunologist Gerald Edelman, who was thought to be a genius and whose lab already contained about a half dozen eager graduate students and at least as many postdocs. I was attracted by his mad intensity, not always distinguishable from mere ambition, as when he told me and another potential student that you're not really doing science unless you find yourself "waking up in the middle of the night screaming."

At first I was flattered to be offered a place in such a popular, state-of-the-art laboratory, and delighted to be assigned to the fashionable study of protein conformational changes, which was my first exposure to chemistry as a three-dimensional undertaking. Proteins are long chains of linked amino acids, folded into specific "conformations," or shapes, that determine their ability to function within a cell, so their foldings and unfoldings are essential to the chemistry of life. But it didn't take long to figure out that I had really been assigned to a machine—the spectrofluorometer that we used to analyze the fluorescent light emitted by dyes chemically attached to the proteins under study, which occupied most of a dark, closet-sized room off of one of the main laboratories. I discovered just how tightly I was meant to be attached to this machine one evening a couple of months into my tenure at the lab, when I was preparing to leave for the day and Edelman stepped into my closet and asked if I understood how much the spectrofluorometer had cost. Because at that price, he explained, he needed it to be running fourteen hours a day at least six days a week, or some other improbable length of time. This is what science had come down to: heads of laboratories getting grants to buy machines that would then come to dictate the research agenda of their laboratories. Why were we studying the use of fluorescent dyes to track conformational changes in proteins? The primary reason seemed to be that we had the equipment to do it, and the equipment could not be wasted. I told Edelman it was Friday night and I had a date and was going anyway, but I left with the feeling that my days of being a free-floating intellect were over, that I had become something more like a machine-tender, or a nineteenth-century mill worker in Lowell.

So when sometime in the spring of 1964 I saw an announcement for the quantum chemistry summer school, I couldn't resist: the exotic setting, the chance to fill in this yawning gap in my chemistry education with a new view of the world expressed entirely in wave functions! Edelman objected, correctly interpreting the trip as a vacation, but I wasn't going to spend my summer in a closet when I could be outdoors or at least someplace absolutely foreign. There wasn't any wilderness in my life anymore, even on the margins, and if I wanted to explore new places I had to make an effort to get to them. That's how I ended up in Istanbul when my mother was reportedly trying to reach me; though I was probably not actually at a lecture on quantum chemistry, which turned out to be even more opaque than theoretical physics, where at least there'd been a few flashes of lucidity. When she was calling me, if she had indeed been trying to reach me, I was most likely wandering the streets of Istanbul, trying to fill the time when the lectures were going on until I could return unnoticed to the dormitory and whatever book I was reading at the time. These walks were challenging in their own way, because I was in no way prepared for the hostility of the Turks once you got away from the main tourist square—the cold stares at my bare arms and ankles, the complete absence of places to sit down, get a snack, or use a toilet. But it was better to walk than to sit and watch the tridents representing wave functions march across the blackboard to a soundtrack of broken English.

Jean didn't know the full story of my dereliction. My crime, since that's how she saw it, was not that I was missing during my mother's crisis. In fact there had never been any understanding between my mother and me that we needed to keep in touch, or even know each other's phone numbers and general locations at all times. If there was a crime here, it was something Jean couldn't have known about and that I only uncovered within the last year, in the course of trying to create a personal/historical timeline for the summer of 1964, also known as Freedom Summer: There was quantum chemistry starting in the middle of August, then the Democratic convention at the end of August. What I had forgotten or somehow misplaced in time was that my mother had come to visit me for a week or so in New York before going on to the Democratic convention. This was to be her only visit during my five years in graduate school, and it would have been my chance to bond with her, to go out to ethnic restaurants and maybe, if the tickets didn't cost too much, sample the emerging off-off-Broadway scene. Maybe I even imagined doing these things with her as a vivacious and only slightly tipsy companion, but when she actually showed up I retreated into my traditional revulsion and arranged to keep our contact to a minimum. I didn't want to drink with her; I didn't want to get trapped by a monologue. So I worked long hours in the lab and devoted most of my evenings to my latest boyfriend, leaving my mother to fend for herself in the local bars or my bare little apartment, where there must have been nothing to do but drink and contemplate her manifest uselessness to the human race.

Jean, if she'd known about my behavior during this visit, would have piled still more guilt onto me. But guilt is a pious sort of emotion, inappropriate to the present cast of characters. As a child I had learned many things from my mother, like how to sew a buttonhole and scrub a grimy pot, but mostly I had learned that love and its expressions are entirely optional, even between a mother and child. No deep mammalian genetic script compels a mother to take a little girl's proffered hand when they step out onto the street. No hormone requires her to respond to an adolescent's teary cri de coeur. My upbringing may have been harsh, but it was also instructive. The idea of a cosmic loving-kindness perfusing the universe is a serious, even potentially dangerous error, and I can thank my mother, however ruefully, for having made that clear long before it was my turn to brush her off.

There is something else that could have contributed to the suicide attempt, an entirely unrelated drama unfolding. During the years when I was in college and without any evident input from actual "Negro" people, my mother had gotten emotionally swept up in the civil rights cause—part of a larger change in her that I saw only in distant outline. She read Thoreau and renounced "materialism"; she mourned Adlai Stevenson's exit from the 1960 Democratic primary to the extent that I, still a vigilant young anti-communist, wondered about her loyalty to America. Then, when she went to the 1964 Democratic convention, she participated in the sit-in to demand recognition for the insurgent Mississippi Freedom Democratic Party. Or maybe she just wanted to participate and was shooed away, whether by the police or the sit-in's organizers, I don't know. She had had high hopes there anyway, for a few days or hours, until the party leaders sold out the insurgents in order to maintain the loyalty of the white southern "Dixiecrats," and it may have been this that sent her down to the pier after dark. Because it is hard to believe that I pushed her in the death direction all by myself.

I flew out to Iowa the day after Jean's call, to visit my mother in the mental hospital she had voluntarily checked into. It wasn't in Ames; I had to fly to Des Moines and rent a car, arriving sometime in the early evening. I expected a chastened and sober mother, or maybe even a cold and angry one, but when I got to the hospital we were immediately joined by some new boyfriend of hers, who I think had driven from Ames, a jolly, buzz-cut guy in the gray suit of an assistant regional sales manager. Never mind the setting or the occasion for our gathering—we all went out to a bar where we drank until I slipped away to my motel and the other two vanished into his car. I don't know what psychiatric treatment modality was in place, but none of this seemed to require any stealth.

Only when I got back from Iowa did I realize how seriously I had lost my way, not just as a daughter or a student, but as the author of my own existence, the leader of my own personal expedition. The quest I had pursued for years had ended in what could be interpreted as disaster or as some kind of breakdown, starting in Lone Pine. Then I had tried to find a fresh mission in science, in particular theoretical physics, and had failed at that. Now that I was toiling at the production end of science, where the big issues are the calibration of equipment and the stability of reagents, I had lost sight of the promised intellectual adventure. I didn't have a quest anymore, I had a job—a place to go in the morning and stay on into the evening, a check coming every month—and what it was all leading to, when I allowed myself to think about it, was at best a lifetime of jobs. I would be a postdoc and eventually a mediocre scientist with a small grant to support my allotted slice of the global research agenda. Maybe I would end up on the faculty of some midwestern university, with an office that looked out on the parched gray cornfields of winter, where I would pine for a chance to travel to a scientific meeting in some place like Urbana or Winston-Salem and present my little crumb of a research result.

There was hardly any sky that winter, or meteorology of any kind, and not just because I worked in a closet. Throughout Manhattan, the sky had been largely bricked off by buildings, and within the Rockefeller complex a system of underground corridors allowed travel from one end to the other without going outdoors. When I did get a chance to look up at where clouds and sun and moon should be, the effect could be startling, leading me to write, for example, the following poem or fragment of a poem:

Child, even this milkiest sky
Sucked by too thirsty
Ascending eye
Will dry, not fold, will crack.
And before it closes you will see
The night outside.

There is no date on this, but it almost has to be from that despairing winter of 1964 when, in the midst of everything else, I was being let go by the older, eccentric, nonscientist boyfriend who had distracted me from my mother's visit during the summer. I knew things were coming to an end at Thanksgiving when he went home to his parents for the holiday, which was no more than a two-hour train trip, without inviting me or even offering an excuse like familial insanity. I had dinner by myself in a diner, buoyed only by the implicit drama, which I imagined I could read in the faces of others, of an attractive girl alone in the neon city on a holiday night. Thanks to my mother, though, suicide was not an appealing option, even as a recreational thought experiment. Where was the dark glamour if you could just get drunk enough to drown, anonymously, in some tacky resort town? If you were going to do it, you had to be clear-eyed and sober, otherwise it was just plain old everyday sloppy death. I wrote to my future self, taking full credit for her existence:

> Forecast: rain for this Friday, December third. But you should know who reads this that I of December third, 1964, the conception [creator?] of your memories and ancestor of your impulse to now read, determined rather not to rain but to sublime, dryly. And so you *are*. I had thought of volunteering for an accident (suicide isn't necessary, it's unnecessarily dramatic, when there are so many accidents, dark mouths of death making little wet sucking sounds when you go by) and they, sensing the thought, reached for me, but I shrank back into the habit of life and so you *are*.

Less than three months later it was my father's turn to make a break for the other side. There is only one written fragment referring to this development, from a letter apparently written to a friend but obviously never sent. The letter is on airline stationery, which was then available in the seat pouch along with the airline magazine, and the occasion for writing was a flight to L.A., where my father had just been in a drunk-driving crash from which survival was not guaranteed:

> Being sucked toward Los Angeles, drinking scotch, reading Genet, inventing an erotic mythology of protein chemistry. My dad smashed up his golden Olds with backseat radio, and probably his life, against a truck. On Thursday night a week ago, when I was vomiting from codeine after dental surgery, his wife [his second wife, Nell] called. She said she's leaving him. Diane [my sister, who was living with them at this point] is seeing a psychiatrist. And now this accident—more accurately, this coincidence of truck and 12-horsepower death wish. "Up to that time, the presence of a phial of poison or a high-tension wire had never coincided with periods of dizziness." (Genet) He may be disfigured, or having DT's, or both.

My father survived that one. When I got to L.A. his face was still cut up like meat, but his blue eyes were intact, staring fixedly into the void that the truck had opened up for him on the highway. I sat with him in front of the TV hour after hour, because that seemed to be what was required of me. He could walk, although unsteadily, but he could not be bothered to speak except for a muttered greeting when I arrived and further mumbles whenever I brought him a glass of milk. His lifelong struggle, it occurred to me now, had not been against poverty, failure, religion, or intellectual backwardness, but against boredom. Obviously we, his family, had never been interesting enough, and I suspect that even his work was insufficiently enthralling. Anything he had ever wanted to learn he could master in a few hours or minutes; nothing was ever challenging enough to tie him up for days or of course make him wake up in the middle of the night screaming. As soon as he had seen the trick, or the pattern, or—in the case of corporate decision-making and preening—the deep layers of bullshit, he was bored enough to need a drink. And of course, once you have that drink, you are not in a condition to ask the follow-up questions that might make even the banal seem mysterious and gripping.

It was dispiriting to see my father like this, practice, perhaps, for watching his eventual decline into Alzheimer's: the blank, hopeless stare, the shuffling gait, the refusal to respond. I wanted his story to contain elements of nobility as well as tragedy, but maybe the real story was not even about him. Maybe it was about alcohol, the "demon rum," or what is more accurately personified as *Saccharomyces cerevisiae*, the yeast that makes alcohol and bread, an ingenious single-celled creature that has found ways to reward us in return for loyally cultivating it. My mother bought packets of it in the supermarket, adding water and sugar to bring it to life when she decided to fill time with bread-making. More commonly, both parents ingested its metabolic product, ethyl alcohol, in liquid form. The result is that just when humans are about to figure out what a great racket this clever little microbe has got going, it offers them a drink and they forget the question. In fact, maybe the whole family drama was just a minor subchapter in the many-thousands-of-years-old epic of *S. cerevisiae*.

But now my father was not supposed to drink anymore, meaning there was to be no escape ever from boredom. Whatever tedium he had entered into—a TV game show, rush hour traffic, a family meal in the kitchen—he'd just have to sit there like everyone else and endure it, or at least that was the doctors' plan. I can understand his despair. There are times when the world just gets too stale to generate new situations and you are left with reruns of what you've already experienced way too many times: *Flight 3647*

to Dayton has been delayed indefinitely. Please remain in the board-
ing area for further announcements.

For the first time since my midteens, I wanted to dissociate, to see the world dissolve back into its constituent elements, and I hoped that the pastel smoothness of the L.A. suburbs could be counted on to get me there. It was time to restir the pixels and start all over again. But no luck. That is not something you can summon as easily as, say, you can order a drink. It happens or it doesn't happen; the choice is not yours. I started reading the Saul Bellow novel my father had been reading before the accident, but it did nothing to lift the banality that weighed down on the house like doom.

How do you distinguish between an accident and a suicide attempt? Surely my father had not swerved to run into the truck, even if he had been dismayed when his wife announced her coming departure. Nor could it be said that he deliberately drank his way to some multiple of the legal blood alcohol level for the purpose of inviting an accident, unless you acknowledge that he did the same thing almost every night. The question of intent was to come up again with a certain forensic urgency after my mother's death eleven years later, from an overdose of painkillers and alcohol. One theory, the most plausible, was that she had simply lost track of how many pills she had taken, ostensibly for a lower back problem, and had slipped gently and of course painlessly from sleep into death. The other theory, advanced by my brother, who had talked to her the day before her death, was that she did it on purpose because she had discovered that her second husband was having an affair. At least she had hinted to my brother that something was wrong. Or possibly, the speculation continued, the husband, who was to remarry not long after her death, had stirred some extra pills into her drinks. There was no investigation, just—

when I went out to Ames for the funeral—a general mood of eva-siveness.

So maybe my mother's covert biographer, the woman who had published a story about us in the literary magazine, was right in discerning a narrative arc that tended toward ruin. The lesson seemed to be that you just couldn't get out of Butte, out of over-crowded little houses and the heat of the mines, without paying a terrible price. Electrons, after all, cannot go anywhere they want; some energy states are not accessible, some transitions are not al-lowed. My family had violated an important boundary of class and geography, for which crime we would all be brought down. I would be the exception, of course: the baby who is tossed from a second-floor window of the burning house and manages to crawl away. If I were a good, responsible person, I would have abandoned my education and set up housekeeping for the wounded, but for-tunately no one was suggesting that I do that.

CHAPTER 10

Joining the Species

At the beginning of "the sixties," meaning in about 1965, news, as in current events, held no interest for me. I didn't have a television or radio, and no source of print news except for the headlines I occasionally scanned at newsstands. If anything happened that might require some sort of action on my part, like an outbreak of plague or nuclear war, I figured someone would tell me about it. It wasn't just that I couldn't be bothered with human events, compared to events at the molecular or atomic scale, because I sometimes enjoyed reading history, especially of the ancient Mediterranean world, where everything important seemed to happen outdoors, at sea or on "windswept plains." What I lacked was the concept of a shared "now." It was hard enough to keep on assembling a personal "now" out of the onslaught of incoming data—the angle of light, the need for lunch, the whispered forecasts of Edelman's mood—although that is our fundamental task as sane and conscious beings, in fact it is what we *are*: momentary juxtapositions of incongruent events. But now for the first time in my grown-up life, history was beginning to intrude into my painstakingly constructed private moment. In answer to the question of what "I" was, I wrote:

> These fragments: the rose, the old lady ridiculous with death and child-size again, the coincidence of me and morning always, almost, repeated, bus stops, headlines, and reverberations of impossible pain. You are the collision of these fragments. Out of many anecdotes, you are a story.
>
> You—who? You in particular, you who are the only one who read of 10 deaths by napalm while the radio was playing "Downtown" and the lady with the white dog walked into the store.

Everyone had their own turning point, when some feature of our shared reality began to seem unbearably insulting or absurd. Mine came about almost incidentally, on a February evening when I was still dutifully at the bench well after nine. I emerged from my closet to find Jack, another graduate student in the lab, still working away with his dozens of neatly labeled test tubes, and we paused to exchange our usual cynical commiserations about the grind. What he did when he was outside my line of sight, which was of course most of the time, whether he watched football games or collected butterflies or hung out in jazz clubs, I had no idea. He was a fixture of the lab as far as I was concerned, with one hand usually attached to some piece of glassware or the dial on a machine—and a friendly fixture in my experience, always eager to explain how something worked or what he was finding out about the heme-bearing protein of horseshoe crabs, which is, interestingly enough, not red but blue. But on this particular night I found him oddly morose. "I don't see the point anymore," he told me. "I'm going to be drafted and sent to Vietnam."

And then I saw Jack—pale, large-eared, good-natured Jack—

lifted out of the brightly lit lab and crouching in a jungle, dodging fire from invisible enemies of his government. I did not have a secure notion of where Vietnam was, other than across the Pacific, but now, with the lucidity of exhaustion, I could imagine a chain, a long concatenation of whorls and loops, suddenly connecting us to this little-known place, and all in the service of some global system of bullying—older men over younger men, white over black and brown, the well fed over the thin and desperate. How had I missed this in all my years of metaphysical questing? Why had I not been drawn to the civil rights movement, which so clearly stirred my mother? For that matter, why had I looked the other way in the last couple of years while my family was visibly disintegrating and my sister, for example, was being passed back and forth from one reluctant parent to another? I don't know, but somehow for me the key to a new kind of awareness lay in this momentary superposition of stolid Jack and the distant jungle. If he could be snatched up into the fighting, then the instruments of coercion were sharper and closer than I had ever noticed before. "But that's crazy," I told him. "You can't go to Vietnam."

The connection between Southeast Asia and the Upper East Side of New York did not of course have to include me. Women couldn't be drafted, nor, as it turned out, could Jack be drafted once the student deferrals were put in place, but that was still many months ahead. When this conversation took place in early 1965, the forces of destruction had already been loosed. The United States had started bombing supply lines in Laos in December; the first American combat troops had been shipped to Da Nang at the beginning of the month. Neither Jack nor I disagreed, at some general level, with the idea that communism had to be stopped. But what if people were so miserable or ignorant that they opted for communism? And if communism meant a life totally managed by government and ruled by petty apparatchiks, what was the difference between communism and the life of a graduate student at Rockefeller University? The war made no sense, and it was possible that the president hadn't been fully briefed. Hence the first political action of my life: Jack and I would write a letter to the president, very logical and polite, explaining why this war would be a waste of American lives and resources, never mind its effects on the Vietnamese.

We got a reply in about two weeks, one of those insulting "thank you for your interest" letters that makes a citizen feel like an intruder. Jack and I conferred and decided we had to acquire more signatories to our letter and especially more grown-up scientists. At the time, this was not an automatic conclusion. I was not in the habit of thinking of people in quantity, as in classes or constituencies, but quantities of *scientists* must certainly matter. The upshot was that I and to a lesser extent Jack, who was antsy to get back to the bench, now had to go from lab to lab, through the many buildings that formed the Rockefeller complex, soliciting new signatures. On a scale of audacity this ranks with a childhood experiment in making earrings—out of shells, from a kit I had received as a gift—and peddling them door to door, only now I interpreted my effrontery as a scientific responsibility. If something irrational was going on, something senseless and deadly, wasn't it my job, as a young scientist, to point this out? Reason, dull quotidian reason, had not gotten me too far in the search for ultimate truth and sometimes even seemed to falter in science, but that was the banner I had to carry now, no matter how numbingly obvious it was, like IBM's motto, "Think."

Our second letter to the president, although adorned with the signatures of some of the nation's top men in biochemistry, phage genetics, and animal behavior, received the same brush-off as the first. The difference was that I had now, as a result of our lab-to-lab signature gathering, collected enough like-minded people to form a "committee"—the idea of a committee being a novelty introduced by a couple of Harvard graduates who were veterans of the early-sixties antinuclear campaign—and begin to plot our next steps. Word of our increasingly organized efforts must have reached Edelman, who took me aside to warn that my sudden turn into activism could lead to charges of "communism." He himself would not sign our letters, nor would any of his immediate subalterns in the lab. His second in command, a gray, middle-aged, beaten-down biochemist, issued the order that I was not to associate with people from other labs, because this was a competitive business and they might be trying to pry secrets out of me—"secrets," I suppose, about conformational changes in chymotrypsinogen.

But it was way too late for me to go back to my original, apolitical state. The war had changed everything. Here we were, doing our usual things—designing experimental protocols, bickering over shared equipment, dashing in at all hours to meet time points—and meanwhile someone, off in a corner, just out of sight, was being kicked to death. We were beginning to get our first images of dead children on the ground, of burned villages and torture in "tiger cages." Just a few months earlier, these atrocities might have inspired in me no more than the distant disgust I had felt when I read Zola's *The Earth* a few years earlier. But now that I had begun to lose the protective armor of solipsism, there was less to shield me from accounts of bayonets cutting through the bellies of pregnant Vietnamese women or napalm-dispensing helicopters swooping down over children. Once the imagination learns how to construct an image of another person's subjectivity—however sloppy and improvised that image may be—it's hard to get it to stop. Anyone's suffering is a potential emergency. Or maybe, as I sometimes thought, I had been hearing the thuds of boots against flesh and the muffled groans of pain in the distance all my life, and just figured out where the sound was coming from.

My political instincts were, and remain, resolutely populist. Since the names of well-known scientists had no impact on the president, we had to get people in quantity, any kind of people who could be persuaded to take a stand. There was no strategic thinking going on that I can recall; our committee would draft a statement that a couple of us—often including my future husband John Ehrenreich—would then turn into a mimeographed flyer for distribution wherever there were people in the streets. Sometimes we would go no farther than the subway stop on Lexington Avenue, greeting the rush hour trains with our wordy, overcrowded leaflets and petitions to sign. Other times we ranged up to Harlem or all the way down to the Garment District, where the streets filled with brown people—Puerto Ricans and Dominicans—at the end of a shift. My approach was serious and respectful: Have you thought about the war? Can I offer you a flyer? Oh, your son is already over there? I learned that the approachability of strangers is demographically determined: A white man in a suit will brush right by you; dark people are usually more accessible; and black women—well, these appeared to be my natural constituency. They might stop and talk, even take some leaflets for friends. I don't think you have ever really inhabited a city until you have walked down the street and seen every single person, no matter how unlikely or different from yourself, how disheveled or foreign, as a potential ally or recruit.

There was an echo here of that delirious early morning in Lone Pine, where I first discovered that the space right in front of me was penetrable by the human body. "The world is plastic in a new way and yields to a look and bends to a voice," I wrote at some point in my early life as an antiwar activist, continuing, more allegorically:

> So far the voice is alone from a high window, which one you cannot tell. The words are indistinct. It is clear what you must do. Must is a heavy word. One day you *had* to buy a rose on the corner and leave that same rose in a subway station. A rose in a tunnel is absurd and also necessary. Necessity meets you on street corners.

I wouldn't have put it so pompously at the time, but I was "stepping into history," sensing, for the first time, that the power of people acting and speaking together could lift us beyond the status of victims or sleepwalkers, and, yes, I said "us." I, the fledgling biologist, was just figuring out that I was a member of a species, part of some vast unfolding genetic plot to transform as much of the earth's resources as possible into human flesh. Because that's what we do: eat plant carbohydrates and animal proteins and turn them into glucose, ATP, and human proteins. Or maybe what I came to understand was more astronomical than biological: that this is a planet, meaning that all of us here are on the same fast-moving rock, suffering, at whatever unconscious level, from the same elation and agoraphobia as we speed through empty space.

At the beginning there was no "antiwar movement," not as far as we knew anyway, only our own do-it-yourself efforts. But as we moved out from the campus into what we called "the community," allies sprang up almost everywhere. I was invited to talk about our committee with some activists in the teachers' and social workers' unions, who turned out to be far better informed than I was, and vastly more experienced about the city, its neighborhoods and networks of potential sympathizers. A group of us went to Columbia to meet with disaffected undergraduates and kept on working with them up to the point when a few of their most prominent activists decided to "pick up the gun" by joining the Weather Underground. I went door-to-door in what were then the slums of the Upper West Side, and when I finally succeeded in putting together a meeting of a couple of dozen residents, the one word I could understand without a translator was "imperialismo." I may have thought I was "organizing," but I was actually being educated and recruited. There were sides in this struggle, unsuspected numbers of dissidents who had been quietly biding their time all along.

I don't think I got nicer in any detectable way, more considerate to family and boyfriends, for example. The ducts that produce the milk of human kindness did not suddenly begin to ooze. Certainly, though, something long denied was coming into play, something for which there are not even good words in English—sociality, perhaps, or solidarity, or a sense of identity with the group. What it had to do with my prior self and her metaphysical quest I didn't have any way of knowing. The conversation that was breaking out all around me was not the one I had longed for as a teenager, in which strangers would run up to one another on the streets and comment on the odd beauty of the world in the face of oncoming death, but it was maybe as close as I was going to get. Large numbers of people, most of them previously unknown to me, were at least willing to admit that something had gone terribly wrong and that the façade of everyday normality concealed ongoing, inexcusable cruelty. We might not be able to do anything about the existential futility, but we might, if we tried very hard, be able to curtail the epidemic of man-made misery.

As other, more stereotypical versions of "the sixties" began to get under way, we drew nourishment from them. We took Dylan's "Like a Rolling Stone" as our anthem—"You ain't got nothing, you got nothing to lose"—moving on from there to Otis Redding and the Rolling Stones. We began to use parties as a means of organizing: Invite everyone you can think of and dance, in any configuration except old-school heterosexual couples, late into the night. Or maybe we were using organizing as an excuse for parties, because we weren't just trying to end the war; we were also trying to start a new and freer and more generous way of life—a goal that put us in some sort of vague spiritual alliance with the counterculture, even if we tended to find the haute tie-dyed and patchouli-scented sort of hippies annoying. I, for one, hated their lazy eclectic mysticism, which seemed to come straight out of the Church of All Religions in L.A. This was not the time to blow your mind with drugs or dissolve into resonance with the cosmic chord issuing from a Tibetan singing bowl. Nor was it, in my case, the time to muse about aberrant mental phenomena and what, if anything, they might mean. There was a war going on, and even we, so far from the actual fighting, needed to be combat-ready.

To fight against a war or, better yet, an entire "war machine," we had to become warriors ourselves. This is the cunning symmetry of war: Enemies tend to come to resemble one another. And this was perhaps especially so in a culture that appallingly—to us—applied the war meme to just about anything, as in the "War on Poverty." More than two decades later, when I set out on a scholarly investigation of war, I was surprised at how familiar the ethos of historical warrior elites already was to me: the willingness to fight to exhaustion and beyond, the readiness to sacrifice all for the cause, even the faint impatience with "civilians." We knew, in the antiwar movement, that no rest was allowed, other than occasional breaks for laughter or dance, because anytime we weren't actively

protesting or building the movement, the real war was continuing and we were implicitly acceding to the slaughter. The trick was
to stay awake and keep on working—drafting new leaflets, planning new outreach campaigns—all the while keeping up with the
lab and scanning the journals in the library. At some point, in the
midst of what I described in my journal as "a muscle-bleeding,
brain-drying tiredness which summons out of some hypertrophied
gland—adrenalin—which raises a false spring-tide in the tissues,"
I understood death in a new way. It was not necessarily a glorious
climax; I was far more likely to die in the middle of things, without completing the task at hand:

> When working too hard, sleeping too fast to dream—rearranging
> things, sorting things, building things, and taking things down—
> and the things, or some thing, murmurs, "Not you is not-this. End
> of sorting, building, taking down. End whether finished. Fore-
> closed whether achieved.

One day, probably in the spring of 1966, I was summoned away
from the spectrofluorometer to Edelman's office. This was the first
time I had been in it, the public space of the laboratory having
been adequate for any previous criticisms, comments, or instructions, and I had no idea what solemn communication might require this spacious, and from my point of view, almost majestic
setting. His face was grave, with the gravity only slightly undercut
by a little crescent of triumph around the mouth. "I know about
your problems with your father," he said, and paused to let that
sink in.

Naturally, my first thought was that there had been a second
car crash, or perhaps some medical crisis arising from the last one,
news of which had just come to Edelman on his personal office

phone. I suppose I asked, but the unfortunate effect of his opening comment was to sabotage the normal process of memory formation. As he went on and it became clear that he knew nothing about my father or his actual problems, that this was all just part of some mind game that was being invented on the spot, I lost track of exact words and sequences. *My father?* What was this man doing talking about my father?

So here was his insight: My "problems" with my father were the source of my "problem with authority." Now, I will admit that I had not taken Edelman's earlier warnings seriously. He was just an odd bird; he even smelled odd, like ozone, as if he were accompanied everywhere by his own personal cloud of ions. If I had been thinking clearly during this encounter, I would have pointed out that there was an upsurge of antiauthoritarianism going on worldwide, from Mozambique to Montgomery, Alabama, none of which had anything to do with my personal family dynamics. I can't remember whether I said anything or whether at any point he explicitly ordered me to desist from my activism and settle into a nunlike concentration on the conformation of chymotrypsinogen. I do recall that he had a lot to say about my abject dependence on him, bolstered by the convenient, and possibly creative, revelation that other faculty members had recommended my expulsion from graduate school and that he was all that stood in their way. Maybe my face was failing to register the appropriate level of remorse and dismay, because what all this led up to was that if I didn't shape up, my career would be over.

The threat wasn't empty, just uninteresting. I'd been in Rockefeller's atmosphere of boiling ambition long enough to see what was actually meant by a "career." It was a wind-up toy, a little drummer in uniform, marching ahead, leading you on, and making announcements like, in Edelman's case, *Nobel-worthy research on gamma globulin! Assistant dean of students! Surprisingly good on the violin!* Did I need a puppet like this to accompany me everywhere I went, opening doors and doing its best to solicit applause? A few months earlier, when I was still committed to philosophical solipsism, I would have found the idea ludicrous, as if I were being asked to go around dressed in whatever spangles and rags other people judged to be my "achievements." Now, however, I was so far from solipsism, so deep into the collective project of the "movement," that the notion of a career no longer seemed to apply. Was I a scientist, an organizer, a street-corner agitator, capable, as I had recently discovered with great trepidation, of addressing strangers through a megaphone? There never was any "career" in my case, just a succession of things that needed to be done, defined in 1966 as whatever the struggle demanded.

It was the part about my father that enraged me, though I still can't explain why this seemed to be such a violation of normal decorum and boundaries. Surely it would have been much worse if he had done some sort of background check and actually knew something about my father—his drinking, his accident, his abandonment of science—and maybe even worse if he had invoked my mother, with whom I actually had "some problems." The insult, insofar as I can pin it down, was the implication that I was a child acting out some primal Oedipal drama, in which Edelman got to take turns with my father in the role of patriarch. How angry was I? There is a poem on a loose sheet of paper tucked in with my journal entries, undated, but most likely arising from this incident:

Knotted on my heart
Insurgent veins
Grasping most brittle wrists
Invasion blushes to the fingertips

Rage builds to flood
And skin contains
In shame restrains
How long?
How long irrigate with salt water this desert?
When the dam breaks: a Red Sea.

I offered no rebuttals and certainly no promises of future obedience. As soon as the fight-or-flight response resolved itself, sensibly enough, in favor of a rapid exit, I left his office, picked up my jacket from the lab, leaving behind the notebooks that contained all my results, since it is the law of the lab—any lab, I suspect—that your work belongs to the boss. Then I walked out of the building and kept on walking—not just away from something, but into something that had always been there, waiting to be acknowledged. The truth was that my "antiauthoritarianism" had come to me directly from my father, who as a boy had declared himself an atheist in largely Catholic Butte, and even in his years of alcoholic decline possessed the most sensitive bullshit detector ever devised. And not only from my father. There was my mother too, whom I could no longer think of without pity and guilt, who risked ostracism with her own atheism and impatience with social pretense, who had sat in, or tried to sit in, with the Mississippi Freedom Democratic Party. And before them both was the great-grandmother who'd thrown the crucifix across the room, the great-grandfather who had refused a job as the mine owner's carriage driver, because that was a job for a servant. So when the sides were drawn up between the powerful and the downtrodden, there had never been any question about where I stood. The flag that I raised in my early twenties had been passed down to me from one callused hand to the next, even if some of those hands were trembling from a hangover or were actually just reaching for a cigarette.

From the day I left Edelman's office—and, it went without saying, my nascent career in molecular biology—you might say that I just kept on walking. Walking was the principal activity of my twenties, not only as a means of locomotion but as an expression of community, even a newly invented form of communication. I walked through Washington with twenty-five thousand other antiwar students in the spring of 1966, the largest number of people I had ever done anything in concert with, all of us polite and preppily dressed so one could mistake us for hippies or freaks. I walked down the middle of Fifth Avenue with another few thousand other people in July in a demonstration that I had, in some small way, helped organize. By the end of the decade, the walks were becoming more dramatic, sometimes turning into runs. I marched up a hill near Fort Dix, in New Jersey, linked arm and arm with a hundred other women who had been similarly selected for sacrifice—right into the waiting line of armed and armored soldiers. When we got within a bayonet's reach of the men, the military police brought out the tear gas and I ended up rolling ignominiously back down the hill, choking and crying. We didn't bother dressing nicely for demonstrations anymore and took to protecting our faces, bandit-style, with cotton kerchiefs.

I even walked up the few steps to the podium at the Rockefeller commencement ceremony in 1968 and received a Ph.D. in yet another field—cellular immunology, thanks to Zanvil Cohn, who kindly took me into his lab after my escape from Edelman's. But to Cohn's chagrin, I took that scroll, which was written entirely in Latin, right out of the world of science and into the great unknown, as proof, I suppose, that I could complete at least one complex and demanding task. After that, the trail gets a little indistinct, leading through a "movement job" that involved editing and investigative reporting, and hence on to what I eventually understood was a new occupation as a freelance writer, which I still didn't think of as a "career," but income tax forms required me to list an "occupation." My real job, as I understood it, was to be a sentry patrolling the perimeters of the human community, always on the lookout for fresh outbreaks of violence and danger, ready to sound the alarm. I became attached to the word "freelance" for its martial connotations.

But the exit from science does not begin to suggest the extent of the transformation I went through in my twenties, a period of time in which, I had once imagined, there would be nothing interesting left to occur. At the beginning of 1965 I had been, except for the succession of boyfriends I depended on to refute my mother's prediction that I would never be able to attract a man, a more or less solitary person. By 1970, I was thoroughly embedded in the affairs of my species—companionably married, a proud socialist and feminist, committed to the betterment, if not salvation, of humankind, always off to one meeting or another.

And in what no longer seemed like a cringing surrender to the reproductive imperative, I became a mother. You may equivocate all you want about the autonomous consciousness of other humans, but when two of them arrive in your life out of nowhere, or out of what had seemed to be fairly inert material, two total strangers, and take up residence in your arms—well, the metaphysical question is settled. They were not notably human when they first appeared, more like fuzzy, pale nocturnal animals, lemurs perhaps, without language or loyalties, habits or traditions—entirely devoted to eating and processing raw sensory data as it came to them. I saw my opportunity at once, which was not to extend my biological self through some sort of dynastic imperialism, but to help them build up a coherent world from the scraps of data that present themselves: "Doggy. And what does a doggy say?" "Bell. Ring the bell. Hurray!" In other words, to rebuild the world for myself, only this time with a couple of brilliant and highly creative collaborators.

So by the early seventies I was a parent and a breadwinner with an ever-expanding political agenda. You can't get much more connected than that. If I were writing an autobiography, this would be the place to start it, with the dense human interactions of adulthood—the love affairs and marriages, the geeky political infighting, the books written and speeches given, the ascent of the children into their own dashing lives of adventure and achievement. Everything I have written here so far would be condensed into an introductory chapter called "Childhood and Adolescence."

But of course this is not the story of me or of that even more imaginative construct, "my life." This is the story of a quest, a childish one, since surely as a grown-up I have not gone around asking, "Why do we die and what is the purpose of life?" But the quest did not end with the onset of "maturity," and nor did its uncanny psychic traces. Short episodes of dissociation kept recurring, set off by familiar triggers like a sudden break in concentration or a compelling influx of light, although I was getting better at snapping out of these states and making my way back to the quotidian without any fuss. I was left, too, with the mystery of what had happened in Lone Pine and later that day in the desert. Did that have anything to do with the altered states increasingly reported by LSD users? Probably not, I inferred from the gaudy psychedelic aesthetic pervading the counterculture in the late 1960s. And why would anyone voluntarily provoke such a traumatic experience? I wasn't brave enough to investigate or at least couldn't imagine finding the time or the setting for a fact-finding "trip."

On the one hand, I was convinced that my perceptual wanderings were a distraction from my mission as a political activist and responsible human being, maybe even a "petit bourgeois" indulgence available only to people who had enough to eat and were not being bombed. (What I didn't know but should have noticed is that the people being bombed in Vietnam were Buddhists, many of them perhaps well along on the route to enlightenment.) My own "epiphanies," to overglorify them, had nothing to do with right or wrong, good or evil, kindness or cruelty, or any other abstractions arising from the human tribal life that I had only recently entered into. Paul's blinding vision on the road to Damascus had come with instructions—stop persecuting Christians and start preaching their faith. My vision, if you could call it that, did not. Whatever I had seen *was what it was*, with no moral valence or reference to human concerns. The steps I had taken toward the morning light in Lone Pine did not lead, through any kind of path, however twisted, to the hill at Fort Dix. There were sides forming up on the great plain of history—the downtrodden against those who do the down-treading, the invaded against the invaders. I had been swept up in this struggle, and from my new perspective, all that was "ineffable" or "transcendent" might as well have occupied another dimension.

There were moments, especially at the beginning of my transformation and before the children arrived, when I wrestled with the suspicion that my new life-among-people was itself a dodge and betrayal of the earlier mission. I had failed as a mystic seeker, or at least given up in mid-project, failed as a scientist, and was left now with nothing I could think of to do except to try to be helpful, soothe the pain, and pick up the pieces in the shared here and now. Ambivalence, maybe even bad faith, runs through the last thing I ever wrote to my future self, which happens also to be dated:

A date, that is a new thing. I write these days against myself, hence briefly; against death, hence at all. The date is a signature I have been embarrassed to sign, to say, "by Barbara—now, or *then*, to [my future self], another dead one, one who by this time you will have betrayed in a new way, another one you abandoned in half-thought, fearing the other half."

I will leave finally a drawer-full of folded papers, letters from one time to another time—letters from a child I buried, and all these letters to it, saying I have not forgotten *you*, but did you ever think of *me*? (i.e., of April 5, 1966)....No, you buried me. Look, you had visions—they are my nightmares and noon terrors. Did you think of me when you practiced seeing, a seeing that sucked the light out of all your tomorrows? Well, you would answer (how well I know the *words*): such tomorrows are the imaginings of other people, and I cannot imagine "others."

I understood that by stepping out fully into the world of other people, I had betrayed my child-self, abandoned the quest "in half-thought." But a few seconds later I am accusing this younger self of dragging me down with her solipsistic madness: *She* had failed to imagine and prepare for *me*. For the next two decades, I stuck to the mental illness line, not that the subject ever came up in conversation: I'd had a bout of schizophrenia as an adolescent, or something like that. I was not sorry to have experienced these things, but I had no intention of returning to them. I knew what I had do. My work was cut out for me.

CHAPTER 11

Return to the Quest

S omewhere in middle age I returned to the quest, or, in its
stripped-down version, the question of what exactly happened there when I was seventeen. In the midst of so much that
was grown-up and responsible—deadlines, campaigns, movements, scholarly undertakings, motherhood—some crucial late-
night part of the ongoing mental churning regressed back to the
events of my adolescence, which were just too *strange*, and I wish
there were a better word, to be permanently buried under the label
of "mental illness" or some kind of temporary perceptual slippage.
"If you see something, say something," as we are urged in train sta-
tions today, and certainly I had seen *something*. Yes, it was
something inexplicable and anomalous, something that seemed, in
a way I could not define, to be almost alive. But this had also been
the case with the oscillations at the silicon electrode, and it was still
my responsibility to report them and bear the shame, if necessary,
of bringing unwelcome, perhaps even incomprehensible news.

The circumstances of my return were not auspicious. The movement that had sustained me for more than a decade was crumbling
under my feet. As my former comrades drifted away, to careers or,

in a few cases, cults or prison, I could no longer imagine myself as a warrior. I was at best a soldier, sticking doggedly to the project of "social change" even when that meant serving in the most tediously compromised fragments of the left, where the idea was no longer to ignite the "masses" but to flatter, and thereby hopefully influence, people who were more influential than we were. More and more of my time was devoted to the feminist movement, but it too was often mired in useless discussion, such as attempts to determine our "principles of unity." I got through the long meetings— often weekend-long meetings in windowless conference rooms— by trying to work out the prime numbers up to 200.

Meanwhile, my father succumbed to Alzheimer's disease, which replaced that brilliant and complicated man with a partially melted wax effigy whose speech was increasingly limited to random word-sounds and chirps. Or maybe it was the nursing homes, as well as the Alzheimer's, that worked this change in him, because if you take away all printed matter, occupation, and conversation, you will eventually get someone who kneels by the toilet to stir his feces with a plastic spoon, or so it has been my misfortune to observe.

Every few weeks I would fly to Denver to visit him, each trip a journey into the unbearable ugliness that humans manage to secrete around themselves out of plastic and metal and short-haired, easy-to-clean carpeting material: the airport, the interior of the airplane, the corporate chain hotel, predictable down to the free cookie offered to each arriving guest. And then there was the nursing home itself. Was I depressed because my father was dying or already dead, depending on how you evaluate these things, or because I had to spend so many hours in a place that made death seem like the best remaining option, if not something to be urgently desired? Moss green and salmon, no doubt thought to be an inoffensive, gender-neutral combination, made up the color scheme, except for the posters serving to remind us of the season—lambs and flowers in the spring, pumpkins in the fall, snowflakes in their proper time. And we needed those reminders, because fresh air was not allowed inside the nursing home, only air freshener.

Earlier, when things were going well, when the movement was thriving and before my father became a shell or my children turned into teenagers, bent on individuating themselves from me as if I represented a potentially contagious condition, I could handle a world without transcendence or even the memory of transcendence. But in addition to everything else, my second husband, who I can say in retrospect was the big love of my life, got eaten alive by his sixteen-hour-a-day job as a union organizer and began to act like one possessed. I had been his eager helpmate—marching in picket lines, going to organizing meetings, welcoming insurgent truck drivers, factory workers, and janitors into our appropriately modest home—but now he was too preoccupied to reliably hear me when I spoke or notice when I entered a room. With my human environment falling apart, the repressed began its inevitable return.

The story of the years leading up to my return to the old questions can best be summarized as a series of measurements and chemical assays: the increase in amyloid protein in my father's brain and the corresponding decline of serotonin in my own; the uncertain tides of estrogen and oxytocin, the diurnal rise and fall of blood alcohol, caffeine, and sugar levels. Simmer all this together for many months and you get a potent toxin, which seemed to come at me in waves. I can remember the luncheon hosted by a countywide women's organization, probably on a Saturday afternoon in late February. All very jolly and heartwarming, until I happened to look out the window of the Long Island catering hall where we were gathered and saw the imminent menace. There was a gas station and an intersection under a pearly gray sky peppered with factory emissions; there was a parking lot mired with the black remains of snow; there was no hope. The award ceremony itself was a mockery, because anyone could see that the people presiding over it were dying right in front of us, if not actually dead, and that rigor mortis had already hardened their smiles into grimaces. And I was not a passive or reluctant participant in this event. I was the one who got the award.

The name for my condition, I discovered, was "depression," which I learned from a 1989 op-ed column William Styron wrote about Primo Levi's suicide. What surprised me was the term, "depression," which seemed far too languid to apply—an insipid "wimp of a word," as Styron himself put it, for "a dreadful and raging disease." I went along with the diagnosis, therapy, and medications, but not without internal reservations. You can talk about depression as a "chemical imbalance" all you want, but it presents itself as an external antagonist—a "demon," a "beast," or a "black dog," as Samuel Johnson called it. It could pounce at any time, even in the most innocuous setting, like that award luncheon or in a parking lot where I waited one evening to pick up my daughter from a school trip. What if her school bus failed to return? What if it had crashed somewhere? Even when I had her safely in the car, it was all I could do to get us home and rush into the bathroom for a fit of gagging and trembling over how close the beast was getting.

It was despair that pulled me back, as a mature adult, to the ancient, childish quest. I could not go on the way I had been, dragging the huge weight of my unfinished project. The constant vigilance imposed by motherhood, along with the pressure to get assignments and meet deadlines, had trapped me in the world of consensual reality—the accepted symbols and meanings, the highways and malls, meetings and conferences, supermarkets and school functions. I seemed to have lost the ability to dissociate, to look beneath the surface and ask the old question, which is, in the simplest terms, *What is actually going on here?*

Or maybe depression in its demon form awoke me to the long-buried possibility that there exist other beings, agents, forces than those that are visible and agreed upon. I wish I could draw some clear lines of causality here, but there are no primary sources to refer to, no journal or even any random notes to my future self.

But when I did try to return to the old questions, very furtively of course, despair and a kind of shame followed me and blocked the way. The impasse was this: If I let myself speculate even tentatively about that *something*, if I acknowledged the possibility of a nonhuman agent or agents, some mysterious Other, intervening in my life, could I still call myself an atheist? In my public life as a writer and a speaker, I had always been a reliably "out" atheist. This was my parents' legacy, and a deeper part of my identity than incidentals like nationality or even class. At some point in the eighties I published an essay-length history of American atheism that unearthed the stream of working-class atheism from which I was descended. I won awards and recognition from organizations of "freethinkers" and humanists. When the subject came up, which it was bound to in our largely Catholic blue-collar neighborhood, I told my children that there is no God, no good and loving God anyway, which is why we humans have to do our best to help and care for each other. Morality, as far as I could see, originates in atheism and the realization that no higher power is coming along to feed the hungry or lift the fallen. Mercy is left entirely to us.

I was no longer the kind of scornful, dogmatic atheist my parents had been. When I read the book of Matthew closely in my forties I was startled by the mad generosity Jesus recommends:

Abandon all material possessions; give all you have to the poor; if a man asks for your cloak, give him your coat as well; and so forth. If you're going to help the suffering underdog, why not go all the way? But then, as the Bible drones on and Jesus fades away to be replaced by "the risen Christ" holding out the promise of immortal life, the message takes on a nasty, selfish edge. How can you smugly accept your seat in heaven when others, including probably some of the ones you love, are confined to eternal torment? The only "Christian" thing to do is to give up your promised spot in heaven to some poor sinner and take his place in hell. Far easier, it seemed to me, to profess atheism and accept the moral obligations a Godless world entails.

As for the mortality that atheism leaves you no escape from—do not for a moment imagine that this was the source of my depression. I was old enough, in my forties, to sense the beginnings of decline, first announced by backaches and the need for reading glasses. What I feared was something more suitable to a depressive: the unthinkable possibility of *not being able to die*. Suppose that my brain had been excised by evil scientists and was being kept alive in a tissue culture medium, then subjected to electrical shocks that varied ingeniously so that my mind could never become habituated to the pain, and that this could be done for centuries, millennia, forever. Or that my body had survived some catastrophic disease, leaving me in a "locked in" condition, unable to move or communicate. If you can imagine these states, then you know that a kindly god would not promise "eternal life." He or she would offer us instead the certainty of death, the assurance that somehow, eventually, the pain will come to an end. Why believers should forgo this comforting certainty, which is so readily available to atheists, is a mystery to me.

My activism required me to be tolerant, to incline my head a

little when others bowed theirs, but all too often I was more challenging on the issue than courtesy allowed, once even picking a
fight with a local liberal minister. He was trying to reassure me that
his vague denomination had no active involvement with God himself and remained fairly open on the question. That wasn't good
enough for me, though. I insisted that the appropriate stance toward an omnipotent God, even the possibility of an omnipotent
God, should be hatred and opposition for all the misery he allowed or instigated. Another time, I disrupted the happy revivalist
vibe at a conference held in a black church because I was tired of
hearing the clergymen who were my copanelists exult in the uni-
fying power of Jesus. I pointed out the number of women in the
audience wearing head scarves, guessed at the number of Jews in
attendance, and announced that I, an invited panelist, was an atheist by family tradition. Somehow I even managed to profess my
atheism to an audience of striking janitors in Miami, all Hispanic
and presumably Catholic or Pentecostal, to the irritation of the
union officials who had invited me.

It wasn't just family loyalty that held me back from potentially
heretical speculations. The whole project of science, as I had first
understood it way back in high school, is to crush any notion of
powerful nonhuman Others, to establish that there are no conscious, subjective beings other than ourselves—no spirits, demons,
or gods. An individual scientist may practice her ancestral religion
with an apparently clear conscience, but once at work, her job is to
track down and strangle any notion of nonhuman or superhuman
"agents"—that being the general term for beings that can move or
initiate action on their own. Thus, for example, the oscillations at
the silicon electrode could not be the work of some malign creature lurking unseen in my lab: That was exactly the possibility that
had to be eliminated, if only I could have found a way to do so.

The same impulse drives me today. If you hypothesize that certain strange noises in the house are produced by ghosts or poltergeists, I will tear the walls down, if necessary, to prove you wrong. Human freedom, knowledge, and—let's be honest, mastery—all depend on shooing out the ghosts and spirits. The central habitat of spirits in our culture is religion, with the excess population flowing over into New Age spirituality, and nothing has ever happened in my adult life to incline me more approvingly to either.

At some point, close to what seemed to be the nadir of depression, I began to dig myself out, using tools that, I now realize, had always been at hand. I was by this time not only a journalist churning out weekly eight-hundred- to thousand-word columns and essays on topical matters, but an amateur historian. The short pieces entertained (and financially supported) me, while the longer historical excursions fed my mind, or rather the insatiable little creature within it that was always demanding fresh questions and fresh clues. Lab work had starved my intellect, but the form of science I turned to now, "social science," which requires no glassware or equipment, opened up a feeding frenzy. At first I wrote books on relatively manageable issues related to class and gender in American society, and then, realizing I had nothing to lose, turned to much larger issues—too large, in fact, for any legitimate social scientist—like religion and war.

I had no reason to think that my new research interests had anything to do with the old metaphysical quest. Anything I dignified in my mind as "work" was about "politics," in the broadest sense, and social responsibility—good, rational, mature concerns that could be justified by my activist involvements and concern for my children's future. But my intellectual agenda was hardly just a matter of rational, liberal decision-making. I had not come out of solipsism into a world of gemütlichkeit and good cheer. To acknowledge the existence of other people is also to acknowledge that they are not reliable sources of safety or comfort.

Metaphorically, you could describe the situation this way: I am adrift at sea for years clinging to a piece of flotsam or wreckage, alone and prepared to die. Then I get rescued by a passing lifeboat, packed with people who pull me in and give me food and water. But just as I am rejoicing in the human company, I begin to notice that there is something not quite right about my new community. I detect uneasiness and evasion in their daily interactions. There are screams and groans at night. Sometimes in the morning I notice that our numbers have shrunk, though no one comments on the missing. I *have* to know what is going on, if only for my own survival. Hence the frantic turn to history: If these are my people and this is my community, I need to know what evil is tearing away at it, where the cruelty is coming from.

I started my study of war and human violence with what I took to be a manageable hypothesis, based on many months of reading, but since I was untrained in any formal or official way, my research method was sheer mania: no stone unturned, no clue left hanging, no disciplinary barrier unbreached. I went from history to literature and classics, I immersed myself in ancient epics, and when anthropology seemed more relevant, I went there, and on to paleontology, archeology, psychology, whatever beckoned. Ah, the joy of libraries after so many years of laboratories! I cannot say that this new phase of research cured my depression, but I learned I could keep it at bay by clinging to the mystery I was trying to solve as if it were an amulet: Get up and make notes on the books that you have, reflect on these notes and order more books, get up again, revise the hypothesis, and figure out a new plan of action. Repeat, making sure to leave no cracks open through which the gray fog of depression can penetrate.

I tested the limits of interlibrary loans from the local public library, and sometimes the patience of the librarians. I got access to a few major university libraries, where I could wander in the stacks, following whatever bat-crazy line of thought turned up. I was in the NYU library, on some kind of paleontological trail that afternoon, when I came across the book that launched a decade of obsession. It was not the book I was looking for, just shelved near it, but the title, *The Hunters or the Hunted?*, lured me in, never mind the esoteric subtitle, *An Introduction to African Cave Taphonomy*, by the South African paleontologist C. K. Brain. The import of the book, which I absorbed in a single sitting, was that you could not understand anything about human violence—war, for example—without understanding that before they were warriors, or even hunters, our ancestors were the prey of more skillful and far better armed nonhuman predators.

Taphonomy is the study of fossilization, and the remains in question were the skulls of early humans, or hominids, found in an African cave. Puncture marks in the skulls had suggested to evolutionary biologists that the hominids had died violently at the hands of their fellow protohumans—an early case of murder, if not actual war. But then Brain came along and determined that the distance between the puncture marks precisely fit the gap between the lower canines, or stabbing teeth, of ancient leopards. I could see no daylight from my desk there in the stacks, no human faces, only the nightmare past recalled, through some inexplicable Jungian mechanism, in my childhood fear of lions. Humans had not written their own history and prehistory, with of course the collaboration of climate and terrain. Our evolution, and even to an extent our history, were also shaped by encounters with dangerous nonhuman animals, especially the larger carnivores, to whom our ancestors were little more than meat. The conventional narrative of unbroken human dominion over the earth and its creatures had managed to leave out some of the central players.

It took a while for me to grasp the metaphysical import of the animals that began to populate my imagination, my notebooks, and eventually my book *Blood Rites: Origins and History of the Passions of War*. Here were the Others, or some of them anyway, whose existence science had tried so hard to deny: conscious, autonomous beings, or "agents" in the largest sense, very different from ourselves and, no doubt, from one another. They were all around us and they always had been. The scientific notion that humans are the only conscious beings on the planet had been an error all along, an error rooted in arrogance and provincialism. Maybe other creatures are prone to similar fallacies: ants, for example, who get so caught up in the politics of ant warfare that they ignore the occasional reports of giant, colony-crushing bipeds.

Since childhood, I had never spent much time thinking of animals in any context, whether as pets or as objects of pity. Modern urban and suburban people live for the most part in an environment devoid of wild fauna larger than squirrels, where you might even forget about their existence except for their curious prominence in children's books and as "stuffed animal" toys. By the 1980s, science was beginning to move toward an acknowledgment of animal subjectivity and emotions, but for the most part educated humans were stuck with the Cartesian view of animals as automatons, driven entirely by instinct and reflex, which is a way of saying that they are in fact, for all practical purposes, already *dead*—just mechanisms responding to instinct and external stimuli. If I had thought anything else, how could I have cold-bloodedly vivisected so many mice in order to "harvest" their cells for my experiments?

But as I got into my late forties and fifties, improving finances made it possible to go on vacations in rural and, incidentally, fauna-rich locations. We started going to the Florida Keys, in the summer when rentals were cheap, and I was struck there by the density of large and even dangerous creatures—snakes and stingrays and especially barracuda and sharks. None of these deterred me from going in the water; in fact, I was drawn by the frisson of being a soft, edible creature among so many experienced carnivores. When I got to know a diver—not a vacationer but a man who dove profession-ally for a treasure-salving operation—I pestered him for predator-related lore, learning, among other things, that it's unwise to bleed in the water, wear sparkly earrings, or "act like a sick fish." I taught myself how to kayak, just barely, and spent hours out in the Gulf of Mexico, finding hot, still spots on the leeward side of mangrove islands, watching out for dorsal fins, and then following—or, as I liked to put it, "hunting"—sharks. No danger in this except for one occasion, when a larger-than-usual shark whirled around at me in annoyance and made as if to ram my kayak.

My next set of vacation destinations, in the Rocky Mountains, brought me within range of more traditional terrestrial predators, chiefly bears. Bears had been a hazard to Paleolithic Europeans, as well as a source of bearskins and, some archeologists assert, iconic images featured in what may have been religious cults. I made my-self into a minor expert on bear attacks, reading all the books available in tourist stores and once following up with an inter-view of the author by phone. The most important thing I learned, from a theoretical point of view, is that bears are not entirely pre-dictable. One bit of lore, for example, is that grizzlies are unlikely to attack a person who is playing dead. But no one should rely on this trick, because sometimes they are attracted to what appears to be carrion. Similarly, you cannot exactly predict where a shark will show up, which could be in a mere foot or two of water where you might have thought you were safe. If animals are reflex-driven automatons, they should obey certain statistical rules, as, for example, mosquitos appear to do when they travel around in a cloud, like molecules of a poisonous gas, but what I learned through observation as well as reading is that large animals are individuals, making minute-by-minute decisions of their own.

Science has been moving in the same direction, and not only because of pressure from the animal rights movement. When observed through a lens cleaned of human vanity, more and more types of animals, many birds included, are found to reason, to exhibit emotions, cooperate, use tools, and plan ahead. I had my comeuppance in the Florida Keys, where I became fascinated by the group behavior of ibises. As the sun sets, they flock to a nearby mangrove island to roost for the night; at sunrise or thereabouts they take off again for their feeding grounds, and I would try to kayak out to watch both events. But the morning liftoff can occur before or at sunrise, and it can be either messy and anarchic or a single, coordinated action involving up to a hundred birds at a time. What, I wanted to know, determined the timing and nature of the liftoff? For surely, I thought, the ibises must be responding to some factor like sunlight or temperature that signaled them when to wake up and fly. Or maybe they were awakened by the sound of fish waking up and jumping. There had to be something—right?—that was controlling their behavior.

But when I put this question to an old college friend and animal behaviorist, Jack Bradbury of Cornell University, he told me essentially that there were probably some leaders and trendsetters among the ibises, but there was also a lot of early morning jostling and nudging. In other words, within certain parameters like hunger and the need to stick together, they do pretty much what they damn well please.

Dolphins are the free-will stars of the seas. You never know when or where you'll run into them, in what season or depth of water, and whether it will be a single one or a pod. I was out on my kayak one day when I noticed some furious splashing off to the north. Paddling to the action as fast I could, I saw it was two dolphins playing some rough, elegant game involving alternating leaps out of the water, and when they saw me, they decided to include me in it. They'd swim alongside the kayak, then vanish under it and pop up dramatically on opposite sides with those wide dolphin grins on their faces. It would have been easy enough for them to flip the kayak over and, if they were so minded, to push me underwater until I drowned, but that was not the game they were playing that day. They fooled with me like this for about half an hour, and then zipped off to find a better player.

I described these encounters to a friend as "religious experiences," and the deeper my studies ranged, the more apt this description seemed. If you go back far enough in history and prehistory, you find humans investing animals, especially large and sometimes dangerous animals, with a charismatic quality, a connection to the divine or at least the occult. Ancient, premonotheistic cultures worshipped animals, animal-human hybrids like Sekhmet, the lion-bodied goddess of predynastic Egypt, or human-shaped deities with animal familiars, like the Hindu goddess Durga, who rides a tiger. Almost every large and potent animal species—bears, bulls, lions, sharks, snakes—has been an object of human cultic veneration. Before the Christian missionaries arrived, my Celtic ancestors worshipped the goddess Epona, who often took the form of a horse. The Makah people of Washington State worship "Whale," who provides them with both physical and spiritual sustenance. If modern people can still get a thrill, as I do, from an encounter with a large and preferably wild animal, it is because such animals once were gods—beneficiaries of sacrifice and the centerpieces of ecstatic ritual.

This posed a fresh challenge to my atheism. What does it mean to be an "atheist" if the gods could be, and once were, so numerous and diverse? I had nothing against Epona or even the death-dealing Hindu goddess Kali, and certainly no way of refuting anyone's claim to have made contact with the Vodoun *loa* or Yoruba orisha in a state of trance. I realized that the theism I rejected was actually only monotheism, or the particular version of it represented by Christianity, Judaism, and Islam, in which the "one God" or "one true God" is not only singular but perfect—both omnipotent and perfectly good and loving. In the Freudian framework, the God of monotheism is a projection based on the child's perception of reliably nurturing and powerful parents. I had no such template to build on, which may account for the scorn, expressed early in my journal, for a "parental God."

But amoral gods, polytheistic gods, animal gods—these were all fine with me, if only because they seemed to make no promises and demand no belief. You want to know Kali or Epona? No "faith" is required, because there are, or were at one time anyway, rituals to put you directly in touch with her. Most of these rituals have been abandoned, repressed, and forgotten, but images of the old gods linger on to amaze us. I was suffering through an episode of deep depression when I got to see the giant chalk horse representing Epona carved into an English hillside. She did not cure me, of course, but I was briefly cheered to think that my ancestors had created an image so expressive of freedom and motion—assuming that all the lifting and climbing hadn't been accomplished by slaves. A few years later I had a chance to visit the great temple of Kali in Kolkata and went down the flights of stairs to the terrifying image of a three-eyed Kali with a long, protruding tongue. She is painted in broad, bold strokes, nothing like the complex curviness I expected from Indian sacred art. She clutches a severed head. Is she good or evil? Does the question even make any sense? I respectfully left her an offering of flowers, as recommended by my Hindu companion.

To propagandists for the one true God, the rise of monotheism represents an unquestionable advance in human civilization. But it can also be seen as a process of *deicide*, a relentless culling of the gods and spirits until almost no one is left. First there was (and in some places, still is) animism, which anthropologists found almost universally among indigenous tribal peoples, although "religion" is a Western notion ill-suited to a worldview in which divine life pervades every single object, animal, breeze, and ray of light. Next, in more complex and hierarchical societies, the divine life that once animated everything gets aggregated into particular "spirits," and eventually into a number of recognized, "legitimate" polytheistic deities. Monotheism is the final abstraction, leaving humankind alone in the universe with the remote and perfect "one true God." Nonhuman animals came to be seen as "dumb" or even evil beasts, best worked to death or consumed as meat. Thus did monotheism pave the way for Descartes and the dead world of Newton's physics.

Where did I fit into this spectrum, or parade, of theological options? Officially as an atheist, of course, the progeny of a working-class lineage that had come to see the "one true God" as a prop for human power relations and his priests as cynical parasites. They were right, these ancestors, as far as I could see, particularly the great-grandmother whose dying act was to throw off the cross that had been placed on her chest. She understood that the great, unforgivable crime of the monotheistic religions has been to encourage the conflation of authority and benevolence, of hierarchy and justice. When the pious bow down before the powerful or, in our own time, the megachurches celebrate wealth and its owners, the "good" and perfect God is just doing his job of legitimizing human elites.

But nonbelievers have mystical experiences too, and mine seemed to locate me squarely in the realm of animism. That was more or less the state of things as I encountered them in May 1959—a world that glowed and pulsed with life through all its countless manifestations, where God or gods or at least a living Presence flamed out from every object. For most of my adult life I had denied or repressed what I had seen in the mountains and desert as unverifiable and possibly psychotic. But thanks to my years of research into history, prehistory, and theology, I was intellectually prepared, maybe as recently as a decade ago, to acknowledge the possible existence of conscious beings—"gods," spirits, extraterrestrials—that normally elude our senses, making themselves known to us only on their own whims and schedules, in the service of their own agendas. In fact, I began to think, edging to this conclusion bit by bit and with great trepidation, that I had seen one.

But what was I going to say? Not that many people were asking, but I was no longer a social isolate or solipsist. I had embraced my species and accepted the responsibilities that go with membership in it, which meant, at the very least, that I could not tell a lie. When the subject of my atheism came up in a television interview a few years ago, I said only that I did not "believe in God," which was true as far as it went. Obviously I could not go on to say, "I don't have to 'believe' in God because I *know* God, or some sort of god anyway." I must have lacked conviction, because I got a call from my smart, heroically atheist aunt Marcia saying that she'd watched the show and detected the tiniest quaver of evasion in my answer.

CHAPTER 12

The Nature of the Other

I t took an inexcusably long time for me to figure out that what happened to me when I was seventeen represents a widespread, if not exactly respectable, category of human experience. For what they are worth, some surveys find that almost half of Americans report having had a "mystical experience," and if the category is expanded to "religious experience," the number is even larger. In a culture where a routine observation can be judged "awesome" or an unusually good meal deemed a "religious experience," I doubt that such surveys have much to tell us except that many otherwise ordinary people have had powerful and unusual experiences for which they cannot easily find words. But every now and then I come across something that rings true to me, such as this, which I should mention is from fellow writer and atheist Daniel Quinn:

> Everything was on fire.... Every blade of grass, every single tree was radiant, was blazing—incandescent with a raging power that was unmistakably divine.... But there was no violence or hatred in this rage. This was a rage of joy, of exuberance. This was creation's everlasting, silent hallelujah.

Of course all such experiences can be seen as "symptoms" of one sort or another, and that is the way psychiatry has traditionally disposed of the mystically adept: The shaman was simply the local schizophrenic, Saint Teresa of Ávila a clear hysteric (although it should be noted that she was also an able and busy administrator). The Delphic oracles may have been inhaling intoxicants; all of the great Christian mystics showed clear signs of temporal lobe epilepsy; indigenous people possessed by spirits are succumbing to "regressive id drives." A recent paper from Harvard Medical School proposes that the revelations experienced by Abraham, Moses, Jesus, and Paul can all be attributed to "primary or mood disorder–associated psychotic disorders."

It's also possible that some reported mystical experiences never happened at all. Paul's vision on the road to Damascus seems sincere enough—at least if it's true that he was temporarily blinded and rendered mute—but later, when he starts boasting to the Corinthians about his ability to fall into trances and speak in tongues, it's hard not to suspect some jostling over status in the emerging Christian hierarchy. I have always been a little suspicious too of Saint Hildegard of Bingen's career-advancing revelation that she should found a convent—which she did indeed go on to do. Between the possibilities of mental illness, fakery, and opportunism, we are on slippery ground here.

There has been a certain amount of scientific interest in mystical states in recent decades, piqued by psychoactive drugs in the sixties and later spurred by the development of brain-scanning techniques showing, for example, metabolic changes associated with prayer and meditation. But for subjective accounts of naturally occurring, as opposed to drug-induced, experiences, the most useful work remains the psychologist William James's chapter on "Mysticism" in *The Varieties of Religious Experience*, now more than a century old. I wish I had found it many years ago, but I acquired the book just in the last decade, and then for narrow historical research purposes, only turning to the "Mysticism" chapter in the last couple of years, when I fell upon it with almost prurient interest. Here are more than a dozen personal accounts of "cosmic consciousness," "the ineffable," even a consuming "fire," and James judges none of them insane or unreliable. In fact, he seems to respect his informants, who include philosophers and psychiatrists, women and men, atheists and believers, and, it has been suggested, possibly also James himself, disguised as an anonymous source.

The accounts vary widely in emotional tone, from reported bliss to terror, but what strikes me on closer reading is that so many of them involve an *encounter* with some other form of being or entity, usually identified as "God," though sometimes more neutrally as "the Infinite" or "a living Presence." Neuroscientists today see anomalous mental experiences as entirely internal events, involving only the interactions of neurons and networks of neurons. In the subjective accounts curated by America's first psychologist, however, whatever happens to a person in a mystical experience does not seem to be the work of that person alone.

I could not seriously entertain the possibility of an "encounter" in my own case until two things had happened. One is that I had emerged, in my early twenties, from solipsism. Starting on that night in the lab with Jack, when I got the idea that there was a mind behind his plain face, when I took the further imaginative leap to sense the human torment behind the headlines, and then, beyond any doubt, when my own children arrived in the world, I came to accept the idea of other minds as rich, complex, and tangled with emotion as my own. Once you have accepted the reality of other human minds, you open yourself up, for better or for worse, to the possibility of still other locations for consciousness, whether in animals or in things normally thought of as "things."

The other development that nudged me in the direction of acknowledging an actual encounter was that in my early fifties I rather abruptly immersed myself in nature. That's a dumb, anthropocentric word—"nature"—implying as it does that what is not man-made is somehow residual, which was far from the case in my new setting. For almost twenty years I had endured the aesthetic deprivations of a lower-middle-class suburb so that my children could go to the town's first-rate public schools. Then the kids grew up and moved out and, independently of that, my second marriage came to an end. I made a midlife dash to Key West, where I had a few friends from our past vacations, and soon took up with a good-looking local who shared my love of the water. We liked our Old Town apartment building well enough, but eventually, worn down by the all-night pool parties in the guesthouses next door, decided to look for a place of our own "up the Keys," where the houses were cheaper and the nights still as death.

The second, and last, place we looked at was in Sugarloaf Key, a patch of land jutting out into the Gulf of Mexico from the lone highway connecting the necklace of islands that make up the Keys. We drove to the end of the paved road, then onto a dirt road cutting through a low jungle of indigenous buttonwoods, poisonwoods, sea grapes, and thatch palms. At the end of that was a pleasant gray house linked to the water by a boardwalk and a dock, and at the end of the dock was a kind of revelation: more than 180 degrees of turquoise water dotted with a series of tiny emerald mangrove islands. *Live here*, said a voice from the blue-green vastness—*whatever it takes*.

It took far less than it might have, because the former owner had the interior decorating tastes of a serial killer. All floor space was occupied by mounds of old newspapers, receipts, porn magazines, and crusty Styrofoam containers. We had the place cleaned out and painted, hauled up some used furniture from a store in Key West, and settled back to savor the gaudy sunsets and try to figure out what kind of a wild place we were settling.

Down in Key West, you can imagine you are in a patch of urban civilization, slightly shiftless and louche, but well stocked with restaurants, supermarkets, gossip, and thick human drama. In fact you could live your whole life on Key West, if you chose, without bothering to notice that you were on an island suspended more than a hundred miles below the Florida peninsula in the middle of the Caribbean. But on Sugarloaf there was no evading the fragility of our existence. Under us, a thin uprising of fossilized coral; to the south, the Atlantic; to the north, the Gulf. Here, you don't think of global warming just as an "issue" but as the vivid, if remote possibility of being eaten by sharks in bed.

The very idea of an Atlantic and Gulf side is a conceit more appropriate to continent-dwellers, because there is of course just one all-surrounding sea. But our side, the Gulf side, a.k.a. the "back country," is different in ways that can make town folks a little uneasy. Before moving up there, I remember talking to a sponger— that is, a man who fished for sponges in the shallow transparent waters of the back country, living for days in his motorboat—and he said a lot about the velvet silence of the tropical nights, the smooth, undulating traffic of the stingrays and sharks. But then he faltered as if there were something he couldn't figure out how or even whether to say it.

I worked, in my usual disciplined, Calvinist way, at a desk facing a wall, but the outdoors was always tugging at me. If your idea of "nature" was formed in, say, the Catskills or the Cotswolds, you may think of it as a kind of absence or quiet, a soothing alternative to highways and cities. But here there was just so much going on, especially in the spring and summer when the water cycle goes into overdrive. All day the sky sucks steam from the warm seas, dumping it back in the psychotic violence of a late afternoon squall, then finishing up with a sweet, consoling rainbow. You might get waterspouts skidding across the Gulf in late summer, miniature tornadoes that mainly bother the birds but can peel off a roof. There may be almost too much to take in at one time— a sunset in the west, the rising moon in the east, a black storm riven with lightning moving in from the Gulf. One July night we stepped outside to find the horizon ringed with at least six discrete lightning storms, each in its own separate sphere of pyrotechnics, leading my friend—a man not known for metaphysical pronouncements—to mutter, "There *is* a God."

Neither of us actually thought it was a "god," but I began to understand that I was being drawn into something, maybe into that very thing that the sponger had hesitated to describe. I came to think of it as the Presence, what scientists call an "emergent quality," something greater than the sum of all the parts—the birds and cloudscapes and glittering Milky Way—that begins to feel like a single living, breathing Other. There was nothing mystical about this Presence, or so I told myself. It was just a matter of being alert enough to put things together, to catch the drift. And when it succeeded in gathering itself together out of all the bits and pieces— from the glasslike calm of the water at dawn to the earsplitting afternoon thunder—there was a sense of great freedom and uplift, whether on my part or on its.

It is not always benevolent, this Presence. Oh, it can be as seductive as the scent of joewood flowers riding on a warm November breeze, as uplifting as the towering pink, self-important, Maxfield Parrish–type cumulus clouds that line up to worship the rising sun. But then, just like that, it can turn on you. I've gone out in my kayak on a perfectly inviting day, only to find myself fighting for my life against a sudden wind and the boiling chaos of the sea. I learned to keep going when survival was not guaranteed, did not even seem likely, by uttering a loud, guttural "unhh!" with each stroke of the paddle as a way of postponing exhaustion and defeat. I was not afraid of dying, because it was obvious that the Other, the Presence, whose face I could almost begin to make out in the foam, would continue just fine without me.

I know the currently popular scientific response to this kind of wild talk: that it is a mistake to see spirits in trees or to interpret certain states of mind as "encounters," and it is, regrettably enough, a mistake that we humans are hardwired to make. But why would evolution favor an innate propensity to error? Here the cognitive biologists invoke the archaic threat of animal predators. Nothing is lost if you interpret that rustling sound in the night as the approach of a lion and there turns out to be no lion there. But the opposite mistake—dismissing the sound of an approaching lion as a wind in the trees—would be fatal.

So, according to the cognitive scientists, our brains are afflicted with a "Hyperactive Agency Detection Device," predisposing us to imagine gods, faces in clouds, divine beings in rocks. This has become, in just the last decade or so, the killer argument against religion, as if we needed another one: that it is an odd relic of our evolutionary history as prey, this tendency to imagine "agents" where there are none. (Though I should mention that the ability to imagine other humans as conscious beings or "agents," rather than as, say, androids, is never attributed to an oversensitive mental "device." *That* ability is deemed healthy and normal.)

What the cognitive biological account tends to downplay, or rush right past in its hurry to get to a thoroughly anthropocentric conclusion, is that there actually *were* lions in the night, bears in the forest, and snakes in the grass. Suppose that of all the mystical experiences reported over the centuries, some actually were encounters with another sort of being or beings. Wouldn't it be wise to investigate? After all, these other beings appear to be, at least for the duration of the encounter, more powerful than a human and at least as awe-inspiring as lions. They can even leave people temporarily unhinged, as I was in the months after May 1959. Saint Teresa reported that her revelations were sometimes accompanied by "great pain" or "an agony carrying with it so great a joy" as to leave one "ground to pieces." Her contemporary Saint John of the Cross likened the Other he encountered in his mystic transports, who was presumably the Christian deity, to a "savage beast." In our own time, the science fiction writer Philip K. Dick experienced a theophany—a "self-disclosure by the divine"—which left him feeling more like "a hit-and-run accident victim than a Buddha." He disintegrated into what was diagnosed as mental illness, to the point of earning a bed in a locked psychiatric ward for several weeks. If only from a public health perspective, we need to know whether there is some sort of etiological agent at work here other than the vague pall of "mental illness."

Here is a humble analogy—some would say too humble and hence completely out of place in any discussion that touches on the "divine." Until a little under two hundred years ago, most human cultures blamed disease on supernatural forces like spirits, curses, or the wrath of God or gods. More sophisticated societies traced illness to imbalanced "humors" or impediments in the flow of qi. As late as the mid-1800s, enlightened Europeans were focusing in on invisible airborne "miasmas" as the source of diseases like cholera. If you had proposed in, say, 1800 that many of the most virulent diseases are in fact caused by tiny living creatures, similar to the "animalcules" detected by Leeuwenhoek's microscope, your contemporaries would probably have judged you mad. It would be like suggesting that the love between people is mediated by a species of very small love bugs.

We forget now, after the easy triumph of the germ theory of disease at the end of the nineteenth century, how improbable the theory must have originally seemed. Humans had thought themselves alone on the earth, except for the animals and any spirits or gods, but we are an insignificant minority on a planet thickly populated by the invisible living beings we call microbes, leading biologist Stephen Jay Gould to call this the "Planet of the Bacteria." Some are benign or even judged to be "good," like *Saccharomyces cerevisiae*, which gives us wine, beer, and leavened bread. Others, like the smallpox virus or *Yersinia pestis*, the agent of bubonic plague, are vicious predators and, some argue, worthy targets for eradication.

Most accounts of mystical experiences—at least of those I have read, which by no means amount to a representative sample—insist that the Other in the encounter appears to be "living" or alive, as in "living God." But is it alive in any biological sense? Does it eat and metabolize? Does it reproduce—an option that monotheism would seem to foreclose? Every now and then a whiff of the biological breaks through the incense-ridden atmosphere of recorded mystical thought. Meister Eckhart, for example, the thirteenth- and fourteenth-century German monk who is often considered the greatest of the Christian mystics, proposed what could be interpreted as a shockingly zoomorphic God, one whose "nature…is to give birth," over and over, eternally, in every human soul that will make room for him. In order to prepare a perfect setting for the divine birth—a sort of nest, or as Eckhart sometimes put it, a "manger"—a person must empty his or her soul of all ego and attachments and turn the resulting space over entirely to God.

The Other who appeared in Philip K. Dick's theophany was even more overtly creaturelike. As related in his novel *VALIS*, in which the author figures as the main character, Dick fought his way back from inpatient status by working obsessively to understand and communicate his encounter with a deity of extraterrestrial origin that is *"in no way like mortal creature"* (his italics). This deity or deities—for there may be at least a half dozen of them in Dick's idiosyncratic cosmogony—bear some resemblance to biological creatures: They have their own agendas, and what they seek, through their self-disclosures to humans, is, according to Dick, "interspecies symbiosis."

Ideally, for further insights into the nature of this Other—its properties, its powers and possible intentions—we would turn here to a vast database of all recorded mystical, spiritual, and religious experiences, not just those of monks and writers but of anonymous adolescents, street-corner prophets, indigenous shamans, peyote-eaters, and so forth. But no such database exists, nor is there any reason to think that an exhaustive one is possible. How could we know what proportion of mystical experiences ever get recorded in one form or another? Maybe the recorded ones are only a small and unrepresentative minority of the total. And how could we correct for the possibility that many recorded experiences have been censored or at least recorded in a form designed not to offend any of the prevailing deities or their human representatives? The intended audience for Saint Teresa's autobiography, for example, was the Inquisitors who were investigating her for signs of heresy, so she may have redacted any visions or insights that could possibly be interpreted as diabolical in origin. The twentieth-century Jesuit mystic and scientist Teilhard de Chardin struggled mightily to imbue his insights with a "Christic sense" lest they be seen as "godless pantheism"—and still his superiors often forbade him to publish.

But we do know enough to say that this Other who appears in mystical experiences is not benevolent, or at least not consistently so. Here I am not talking about the monotheistic God, or whatever entity can be blamed for natural disasters and birth defects—just about that Other whose existence could be inferred· from reported mystical experiences or, for that matter, from close attention to natural phenomena like tropical weather. The early-twentieth-century theologian Rudolf Otto surveyed the works of (mostly Christian) mystics for clues as to the nature of the *mysterium tremendum*, as he termed it, a.k.a. the "Wholly Other," and concluded that it was "beyond all question something quite other than the 'good.'" It was more like a "consuming fire," he said, perhaps from personal experience, and "must be gravely disturbing to those persons who will recognize nothing in the divine nature but goodness, gentleness, love, and a sort of confidential intimacy." As Eckhart, one of Otto's many sources, had asserted centuries earlier, referring to the Other as "God," the religious seeker must set aside "any idea about God as being good, wise, [or] compassionate."

This of course poses a nearly insoluble problem: Mysticism often reveals a wild, amoral Other, while religion insists on conventional codes of ethics enforced by an ethical supernatural being. The obvious solution would be to admit that ethical systems are a human invention and that the Other is something else entirely. After all, human conceptions of morality derive from the intensely social nature of the human species: Our young require years of caretaking and we have, over the course of evolution, depended on one another's cooperation for mutual defense. Thus we have lived, for most of our existence as a species, in highly interdependent bands that had good reasons to emphasize the values of loyalty and heroism, even altruism and compassion. But why should a being whose purview supposedly includes the entire universe share the tribal values of a particular group of terrestrial primates? The God of religion, the enforcer of ethics, is one thing, the "Wholly Other" revealed in mystical experiences quite another.

Otto, good Protestant that he was, refused to make this distinction. Religions, especially of the highest, so-called world religion rank, seem to require their founding revelations—annunciations, Damascene moments, visits from Allah in a cave—to convince us of their nonhuman, "divine" origin. Presumably the Hebrews would not have accepted the Ten Commandments if they came in the form of a memo. The commandments had to be delivered by a bearded prophet whose mystic credibility had been conferred by the burning bush and who came down from the mountain accompanied by a terrifying display of thunder and lightning. Somehow human authority is never enough; we must have special effects. Otto, too, wanted his Christian ethics to be grounded in the "numinous" as glimpsed by the mystics, so he perpetuated the confusion. Even some of our more scientifically grounded philosophical thinkers today, like the Canadian philosopher John Leslie, struggle mightily to detect some ethical principle infusing the natural world.

If the Other as perceived by mystics is not benevolent, neither is it necessarily malevolent; in fact both descriptions are flagrantly anthropocentric. Why should it be "for" us or "against" us any more than the God of monotheism should favor the antelope over the lion? A creature of some kind, an alternative life form, as suggested by Dick, would have its own agenda, sometimes working to our advantage and sometimes against us—as in the lowly case of *E. coli*, which plays an important role in human digestion but can also be an agent of mortal illness—but we do not know what that creature is, if "creature" is even the right word.

Barred from more respectable realms of speculation, the idea of a powerful invisible being or beings has been pretty much left to the realm of science fiction, where, as it happens, I spent some of the happiest hours of my youth. In some classic sci-fi, the being in question is a god or a kind of god. Olaf Stapledon's 1937 novel *Star Maker*, for example, ends with its far-traveling human protagonist finally encountering the eponymous "eternal spirit," who has been allowing one planetary civilization after another to flourish and die out, for no evident reason: "Here was no pity, no proffer of salvation, no kindly aid. Or here were all pity and all love, but mastered by a frosty ecstasy." In Arthur C. Clarke's short story "The Nine Billion Names of God," Tibetan monks who have set themselves the task of generating all the possible names of God finally get some assistance from a computer brought to them by Western technicians. As the technicians make their way back down the mountainside from the monastery, they look up at the night sky to see that, "without any fuss, the stars were going out." The monks had been right: The universe existed for the sole purpose of listing the names of God, and once this exercise in divine vanity was accomplished, there was no reason for the universe to go on.

Clarke's novel *Childhood's End* more fully develops the theme of an über-being that uses humans for its own inscrutable purposes. Clark was no New Age fluffhead; he was an avowed atheist with a background in physics and rocket science. Yet the plot centers on an unseen "over-mind" of remote extraterrestrial provenance, which sends its agents to essentially domesticate humankind. War is ended, along with many of the more obvious forms of injustice, leading to an era of peace and harmony that Clarke, with typical Cold War contempt for utopias, portrays as comfortable but dull. Meanwhile, the over-mind's agents seek out the more mystically adept members of humanity, who are eventually recruited into a kind of trance culminating in mass spiritual unity with the over-mind. When that has been achieved, the earth blows itself up, along with the last human on it, after which the over-mind presumably moves on to find a fresh planet—and species—to fulfill its peculiar cravings.

Science fiction, like religious mythology, can only be a stimulant to the imagination, but it is worth considering the suggestion it offers, which is the possibility of a being (or beings) that in some sense "feeds" off of human consciousness, a being no more visible to us than microbes were to Aristotle, that roams the universe seeking minds open enough for it to enter or otherwise contact. We are not talking about God, that great mash-up of human yearnings and projections, or about some eternal "mystery" before which we can only bow down in awe. I have no patience with Goethe when he wrote, "The highest happiness of man is to have probed what is knowable, and to quietly revere what is unknowable." Why "revere" the unknowable? Why not find out what it is?

Science could of course continue to dismiss anomalous "mystical" experiences as symptoms of mental illness, but the merest chance that they represent some sort of contact or encounter justifies investigation. After all, rational people support SETI, or the Search for Extraterrestrial Intelligence, despite what is so far a resounding silence from the skies. Similarly, scientists prowl the earth looking for "weird life," meaning not just the "extremophiles" that inhabit hot springs and glaciers, but organisms that may be based on silicon instead of carbon or arsenic instead of phosphorus. It is not unscientific to search for what may not be there—from intelligent aliens to Higgs bosons or a vast "theory of everything" underlying all physical phenomena. It is something we may be innately compelled to do.

The fact that this being or beings is so far undetectable to us and our instruments does not mean that it is made out of some supernatural "mind-stuff" unlike familiar matter and energy (not,

I should note, that "familiar" matter and energy any longer seem to comprise very much of the "stuff" in the universe). Whether this being is alive, in a biological sense, as Dick proposed, is of course entirely conjectural, if only for the simple taxonomic reason than that biologists themselves are not agreed on a definition of life: Does life involve metabolism, meaning eating and respiring, or is it enough to be able to reproduce, as in the case of viruses? Monotheism inhibits us from imagining anything involved with the "numinous" or "holy" as part of a *species*, since a species generally has more than one member. But if the hypothesized beings are "alive," that is, technically speaking, what we are dealing with.

As for those who insist on a singular deity, I would note that the line we draw between an individual and a multitude is not always clear: Slime molds can exist as individual cells or join together to form a single body; bacterial colonies can exhibit a kind of intelligence unavailable to individual bacterial cells. Humans can live alone or in small clusters and then suddenly, in the face of a common enemy, band together and begin to act like a single unit, which in turn just as readily disperses. If there seems to be some confusion here on the subject of case—whether to say Other or Others, deity or deities—it grows out of the limits of our biological imagination.

One possible biological analogy for the relationship between humans and the Other or Others would be symbiosis, as Dick proposed. This is the kind of relationship that exists between humans and the trillions of microbes that inhabit our guts. The microbes get a comfortable place to live, regularly bathed in nutritious fluids; the human gets digestive assistance, some defense against foreign bacteria, and useful microbial products like vitamin K. To scale up, rather joltingly, from intestinal flora to the God of monotheism, there have even been suggestions that he exists in a symbiotic relationship to humans. The twentieth-century theologian Abraham Heschel wrote that Jewish mystics were historically "inspired by a bold and dangerously paradoxical idea that not only is God necessary to man but man is also necessary to God, to the unfolding of his plans in this world," although Heschel gives us no reason to suspect that God's plans are in any way biologically self-serving.

There are far uglier possible relationships between disparate species. When I was a girl just setting out on my quest, I asked myself whether I would want to know the "truth" even if I was given the "foreknowledge that it would only be a bitter disillusionment." This possibility had been impressed on me at a very young age by a radio drama, long ago, when there were such things in America, with actors and scripts. Four mostly paralyzed veterans occupy a hospital room, where only one can see out the window. He whiles away the hours by describing the outside world to his roommates—the comings and goings, the laughing children, the pretty girls—until one of the other men demands that *he* get a turn in the bed by the window. The switch is made. The new guy gets the window and discovers that what actually lies outside is nothing but a brick wall—no comings and goings, no laughter or sunshine. Would I want to know a truth like that? Courageously, or so I thought at the time, I decided that I would.

Well, here it is: The worst possible relationship between humans and some mystically potent being or beings, at least the worst that I can imagine, would be not symbiosis but parasitism. Plenty of familiar creatures cannot live on their own; they require hosts, and, interestingly, some of them are capable of modifying the behavior, and possibly also the thoughts and feelings, of their hosts. For example, a flatworm, *Leucochloridium paradoxum*, infects normally shade-loving snails and prompts them to crawl into the sunlight where they may be eaten by a bird, which then becomes the flat-worm's next host. A parasitic wasp compels its spider host to spin an unnatural kind of web that will be used to house the wasp's progeny, not the spider's. Some parasites even manufacture hormones and neurotransmitters that can act on their hosts, perhaps even inducing an insect version of ecstasy. Certainly the highly asymmetrical arrangement proposed by Eckhart—between a relentlessly procreative God and the humans who serve as its hosts—looks very much like parasitism. If so, those who think of themselves as "enlightened" may in fact have been infected and, in some hideously intimate way, *used*.

Do I believe that there exist invisible beings capable of making mental contact with us to produce what humans call mystical experiences? No, I *believe* nothing. Belief is intellectual surrender; "faith" a state of willed self-delusion. I do not *believe* in the existence of vampire-spirit-creatures capable of digging deep into our limbic systems while simultaneously messing with our cognitive faculties, whether we experience the result as madness or unbearable beauty. But experience—empirical experience—requires me to keep an open mind. And human solidarity, which is the only reason for writing a book, requires that I call on others to do so also.

There are other possibilities than "creatures" or "beings" of any kind. Science has always wrestled with the idea of an immaterial will, or agency, at work in the universe, and for centuries it was thought to be expressed through the "laws of nature." God might be dead, but he rules on, or so it was thought, through his immutable laws. It turns out, however, that those laws are at best crude averages, rough generalizations. Take a more fine-grained look, or develop more sensitive instruments, and things get more interesting. At the smallest, quantum, level, there are no laws at all, only probabilities. An electron can be here, there, or both places at once, very much as if it had a choice in the matter. At the macroscopic level, the meteorologist Edward Lorenz found that rounding off the number .506127 to .506—for simplicity, and because of the crudeness of his computer—he came out with wildly different weather predictions: the so-called butterfly effect. This is not to say that electrons make reasoned decisions or that winged insects govern the weather—just that the natural world has gotten a lot livelier than it was when I first came on the scene as a young student of science.

A hint of—dare I say?—*animism* has entered into the scientific worldview. The physical world is no longer either dead or passively obedient to the "laws." It can surprise us, as for example, when an electron-positron pair springs out of total vacuum, an ordinary summer storm whips itself into a tornado, or a simple circuit develops the power to oscillate. Nothing supernatural is involved in any of these cases; even the oscillating electrode is following old-fashioned laws of electrodynamics. It's just following them in ways we could not have predicted, ways that give rise to an "emergent" pattern that seems to come out of nowhere. As for the emergence of matter out of nothing, which tormented me so much as a child, we are coming to see that there *is* no Nothing. Even the most austere vacuum is a happening place, bursting with possibility and constantly giving birth to bits of Something, even if they're only fleeting particles of matter and antimatter. To quote the polymathic and determinedly rationalist Howard Bloom, "We have vastly underrated the cosmos that gave us birth. We have understated her achievements, her capacities, and her creativity. We've set aside will, purpose, and persistence in a magic enclosure and have claimed that…[they] do not belong to nature, they belong solely to us human beings."

We have, in other words, made ourselves far lonelier than we have any reason to be. My adolescent solipsism is incidental compared to the collective solipsism our species has embraced for the last few centuries in the name of modernity and rationality, a worldview in which there exists no consciousness or agency other than our own, where nonhuman animals are dumb mechanisms, driven by instinct, where all other deities and spirits have been eliminated in favor of the unapproachable God of monotheism, a worldview in which, as the famed twentieth-century biochemist Jacques Monod put it, "Man at last knows he is alone in the unfeeling immensity of the universe." If I was, when I entered adulthood, a little bit nuts, it was because I was struggling to fully accept that view of the world.

For all that I had learned since middle age about science and new science, religion and the old religion, I would never have committed myself to the project that became this book if not for a couple of disasters. First was the cancer that disposed me to thoughts of imminent mortality at exactly the time I was sorting through my papers with a librarian in 2001. I was prepared to die, at least as the freakish older person I had become, bald and enfeebled by the cancer treatments, but I was not ready to let go of my younger self, which is why I snatched up my journal and saved it from permanent incarceration in a library basement.

Still, I was not moved to any kind of follow-up for another four years, and then only by an "act of God." By this time I had more or less relocated to the mainland, with the intention of selling my house in the Keys. Then, in October 2005, a few weeks after the far more catastrophic Katrina, Hurricane Wilma struck the Keys, generating a storm surge five feet high. When I traveled down a few weeks after the storm to survey the damage, bringing along friends to help with salvage and repair, I discovered that most of the evidence of my existence—the paper traces anyway—had been swept away. My study, located at ground level, was a soggy ruin, already encrusted with mold. This was my Ozymandias moment: Gone were the files containing all the articles I had ever published, financial records, computer disks, along with the books I was using for the research I was doing at the time.

My journal survived only because, in some uncharacteristic act of foresight, probably at the time of the librarian's visit in 2001, I had moved it to a second-floor storage space, where the flood was not able to find it. When I flew back to where I was living near my daughter and grandchildren in Virginia, the journal came with me in my carry-on bag, and shortly after my return I dismissed the last of my male companions for a number of compelling reasons, topped by my need to be alone, which had become far more urgent than any romantic attraction. Then, in the midst of so many other serious and worldly obligations, I began to transcribe the journal, a few hours a day for a couple of weeks, and eventually coming across the question I had addressed to my older self when I was about sixteen: "What have you learned since you wrote this?"

This is the challenge that comes hurtling out at me from across the decades like a final exam or an exit debriefing: What have I learned? And of course it does not mean what did I learn about protein conformational changes or military history or even about the roots of systematic human cruelty and how we could go about creating kinder social arrangements. It means, *What did you learn about all of this? What is going on here? Why is this happening?*

Well, I have to admit to my child-self: not enough, not anywhere near enough. To please you I would have had to devote my life to neuroscience and philosophy, possibly also ashrams and spiritual discipline. I would have studied cosmology and math. I would have passed many hours with fellow seekers, perhaps in scenically magnificent settings, debating, sharing, comparing. But I came of age in a time of turmoil and, naturally enough, I took a side. The time I could have spent carrying on the quest went instead into meetings and protests; my research interests turned to wages and poverty, war and the mechanisms of social change. I would not expect my sixteen-year-old self to understand this redirection, she who did not even fully acknowledge the autonomous existence of other human beings. But this is how it turned out: I fell in love with my comrades, my children, my species.

I learned this much, though, which, given the poverty of metaphysical speculation in our time, an atheist admits only at some risk to her public integrity: You first have to revise the question. To ask *why* is to ask for a motive or a purpose, and a motive has to arise from an apparatus capable of framing an intention, which is what we normally call a *mind*. Thus the question *why* is always really the question *who*.

Since we have long since outgrown the easy answer—God—along with theism of any kind, we have to look for our *who* within what actually exists. No one is saying that the universe, as an entity, is alive, and certainly not that it has motives or desires. But the closer and more carefully we probe, the more it seethes with what looks like life—runaway processes driven by positive feedback loops, emergent patterns, violent attractions, quantum leaps, and always, as far ahead as we can see, more surprises. There may be no invisible creaturely "beings" afoot, either symbionts, parasites, or predators. But there are uncountable algorithms at work in the physical world, writhing and reaching, pulling matter and energy into their schemes, acting out of what almost seems to be an unquenchable playfulness. Sometimes, out of all this static and confusion, the Other assembles itself and takes form before our very eyes.

In my case, this continues to happen right up to the present, although mercifully in much less cataclysmic form than when I was a teenager. Just a few days ago, for example, I found myself downtown a little after noon in a grassy space lined with food trucks. I wasn't hungry but I wasn't in a rush to get anywhere either, so I fell into the line for one of the trucks, attracted by the great flow of people out of their office buildings queuing up patiently as if for the distribution of some sort of blessing. It was the first genuinely springlike day of the season, sunny and disheveled. As I got closer to the truck I had chosen to wait in line for, my eye was caught by something inside it, semicircular and brassy, maybe a knob or a handle, gleaming with its own personal supply of sunlight, and I lost it there for a moment, stunned by the audacity of this object trying to condense the light of a star into its little circumference, stunned by the whole arrangement—buildings, lines, trucks—like some paleoastronomical structure designed to capture the first rays of the solstice sunrise so that the ceremony can begin, the mass inpouring and outpouring of ecstasy from the heavens and back...

Ah, you say, this is all in your mind. And you are right to be skeptical; I expect no less. It *is* in my mind, which I have acknowledged from the beginning is a less than perfect instrument. But this is what appears to be the purpose of my mind, and no doubt yours as well, its designated function beyond all the mundane calculations: to condense all the chaos and mystery of the world into a palpable Other or Others, not necessarily because we love it, and certainly not out of any intention to "worship" it. But because ultimately we may have no choice in this matter. I have the impression, growing out of the experiences chronicled here, that it may be seeking us out.

ACKNOWLEDGMENTS

I thank the family members who helped fill in historical details—Ben Alexander, Nell Babcock, and especially Diane Alexander, who also commented on an earlier draft. I am grateful to physicist Ron Fox for trying to explain nonlinear dynamics and to anthropologist Janet McIntosh for so many gripping conversations over the years and, in particular, for introducing me to cognitive biology. Along the way, I also had useful exchanges with Howard Bloom, Rosa Brooks, Ben Ehrenreich, Arlie Hochschild, Adam Green, Bernard Schweizer, and George Sciallaba.

My agent Kris Dahl pressed me to turn what was originally conceived as a history of religion into a personal narrative. At first I resisted, but I think that, as usual, she was right. Deb Futter, my ebullient editor at Twelve, provided insightful comments and a level of enthusiasm that pulled me through the usual bouts of writerly despair. Sara Holloway did a challenging, masterful, line-by-line edit. Many other people had a hand in the making of this book and I am particularly grateful to Brian McLendon, Libby Burton, Roland Ottewell, who copyedited it, and Catherine Casalino, who oversaw the cover design.

ABOUT THE AUTHOR

BARBARA EHRENREICH is the author of fourteen books, including the bestselling *Nickel and Dimed* and *Bait and Switch*. She lives in Virginia.

ABOUT TWELVE
MISSION STATEMENT

TWELVE was established in August 2005 with the objective of publishing no more than one book per month. We strive to publish the singular book, by authors who have a unique perspective and compelling authority. Works that explain our culture; that illuminate, inspire, provoke, and entertain. We seek to establish communities of conversation surrounding our books. Talented authors deserve attention not only from publishers but from readers as well. To sell the book is only the beginning of our mission. To build avid audiences of readers who are enriched by these works—that is our ultimate purpose.

For more information about forthcoming TWELVE books, you can visit us at www.twelvebooks.com.